CLEARING THE PATH

CONNECTING WITH GOD IN A CLUTTERED WORLD

NATHAN WESTWICK

WestBow Press
A DIVISION OF THOMAS NELSON
& ZONDERVAN

Copyright © 2023 Nathan Westwick.

All rights reserved. No part of this book may be used or reproduced by any means, graphic, electronic, or mechanical, including photocopying, recording, taping or by any information storage retrieval system without the written permission of the author except in the case of brief quotations embodied in critical articles and reviews.

This book is a work of non-fiction. Unless otherwise noted, the author and the publisher make no explicit guarantees as to the accuracy of the information contained in this book and in some cases, names of people and places have been altered to protect their privacy.

WestBow Press books may be ordered through booksellers or by contacting:

WestBow Press
A Division of Thomas Nelson & Zondervan
1663 Liberty Drive
Bloomington, IN 47403
www.westbowpress.com
844-714-3454

Because of the dynamic nature of the Internet, any web addresses or links contained in this book may have changed since publication and may no longer be valid. The views expressed in this work are solely those of the author and do not necessarily reflect the views of the publisher, and the publisher hereby disclaims any responsibility for them.

Any people depicted in stock imagery provided by Getty Images are models, and such images are being used for illustrative purposes only.
Certain stock imagery © Getty Images.

Unless marked otherwise, all scripture quotations are taken from The Message. Copyright © 1993, 1994, 1995, 1996, 2000, 2001, 2002. Used by permission of NavPress Publishing Group.

Scripture quotations marked NLT are taken from the Holy Bible, New Living Translation, Copyright © 1996, 2004, 2015 by Tyndale House Foundation. Used by permission of Tyndale House Publishers, Inc., Carol Stream, Illinois 60188. All rights reserved.

Scripture quotations marked NIV are taken from The Holy Bible, New International Version®, NIV® Copyright © 1973, 1978, 1984, 2011 by Biblica, Inc.® Used by permission. All rights reserved worldwide.

ISBN: 979-8-3850-0066-1 (sc)
ISBN: 979-8-3850-0067-8 (hc)
ISBN: 979-8-3850-0068-5 (e)

Library of Congress Control Number: 2023910811

Print information available on the last page.

WestBow Press rev. date: 8/9/2023

CONTENTS

Foreword ix
Introduction xiii

Chapter 1 – Thunder in the Desert:
    Prepare the Way for the Lord (Part 1) 1

Chapter 2 – Thunder in the Desert: Prepare the Way
    for the Lord (Part 2) 7

Chapter 3 – Fill Those Valleys 17
    Filling the Valleys 21
    The Innocuous Fillers 23
    The Harmful Fillers 26
    A Word about Valleys–They Start Easy 29
    Some Practical Ways to Climb Out 30
    Now Let's Fill those Valleys 32

Chapter 4 – Bulldoze Those Hills! 35
    Identification 37
    Confession 42
    Change 46
    It's a Heart Thing 48
    A Word about Our Pain, Trauma, and Injuries 52
    A Note about the Bulldozed Hills 55

Chapter 5 – Filling the Ruts 57
    Examining Our Habits 60
    Examining Their Value 62

Eliminate the Minuses 65
Some Spiritual Practices to Try 66
   Regular Bible Reading 70
   Silence 71
   Listening Prayer 72
   Fasting 76
   Worship 81
   Solitude and Retreat 83

Chapter 6 – Work Tirelessly to Remove the Rocks 85
Ask God to Reveal the Rocks 88
Rocks That Originate from Our Fear 91
   Our Tendency to Take Control 95
Rocks that Stem from Our Misunderstanding of Identity 98
A Few Tools to Offer 101
   Identify 101
   Crucify 102
   Sanctify 108
In Summary 111

Chapter 7 – The Identity of God 117
Let God Speak for Himself 123
God is Powerful over Nature 124
God is Powerful over Governments 125
God is Powerful over _____ 126
God is Nurturing 127
God Doesn't Abandon Us 129
God Has Been There since the Beginning and Will Be
There through the End 135
God Gives Us Strength 136

Chapter 8 – Your True Identity 141
God is Central 144
God Gives Us Our Identity 148
Invite God into the Process 151
How This Affects Us 154

Chapter 9 – What's Next? 159
    Abiding 160
    When We Abide 164
    Back to Identity 165
    Back to the Beginning 166

Chapter 10 – Conclusion 169
    More on Emmanuel 169
    Walking In the Clear Path 174

Benediction 177
Afterword 179
Acknowledgments 185
About the Author 189

FOREWORD
by Matthew Brown

When I gave my life to Christ in my early 20s, I had a new spirit, a new life, and I was eager to walk a new path. I was ready, and I mean really ready, to leave my life of sin and cling to Jesus. I thought I had all the desire I would need to follow Christ and was prepared to take on the challenges of a real life committed to my faith. But I was unprepared for the immensity of the obstacles I would face and the extreme duration of my journey. Being a young man, I lived in the now and was naive to the fact that God worked in the eternal. I was ready to die for Jesus but not live a lifetime with Him.

In one of Jesus' most important teachings, He reminds us that the road that leads to life is narrow and that few find it. I had found it but struggled to stay on it. There is a difference between knowing the path and actually walking it. Jesus is easy to find but hard to follow. The path that He has carved out for us is not just narrow but difficult. The road has potholes, slippery gravel, and cliffs on each side. Sometimes there are mountains to move and valleys to fill. It has been a miracle, and through the grace of God, that I have stayed on this path. Sadly, many of my fellow disciples have fallen away. What I have barely been able to handle has swallowed many of my sincere friends in the faith.

Salvation is about choosing the right path; sanctification is about clearing that path. Christ was crucified for your sins, but the path can make you feel like you are the one being crucified. I wish there was a book like Nate Westwick's when I started—something to help me work through the natural obstacles of life and the supernatural barriers that a spiritual life must overcome. The Christian life is not easy, but it is worth it. Jesus has done the work for your soul, but you must do the work for your walk.

One of the first verses I memorized as a young Christian was 1 John 2:6, "Whoever claims to know him must walk as Jesus did." To know Jesus is to walk like Jesus and to live like Him. According to Luke 2:52, Jesus grew in three specific ways. He grew in relationship with Himself, God, and others. You will also need to master all three ways if you want to stay squarely on the path.

Notice that Luke records that Jesus grew first in relation to Himself. Many believers fail to consider the role of self on their individual spiritual journey. They will say it's all about God, which it is. But God will never be the hindrance to your walk. You will. Your sinful desires and your brokenness from the wounds of others and from life will cloud your vision and hinder your walk. If you do not grow through these things, you will not become better—only bitter. Bitterness is the road that will lead you off of the path that God has for you. Better is the Luke 2:52 path. As you follow Jesus, you must get to know yourself. Your lack of self-knowledge will be the biggest barrier to gaining real knowledge and insight into God. If you truly want to know God, you must know yourself.

I realize this may feel defeating, but remember; you are not alone. Jesus is with you, and you will need Him every step of the way. You will also need wisdom in navigating the treacherous steps of a follower of Jesus. That is where *Clearing the Path* is so helpful. This book will help you identify problems and discover solutions to "clearing the path" so God can truly work in your life.

I have known Nate Westwick for decades. When we first met, we were both naive about the challenges of following Jesus. Over the years, other believers have deeply hurt us, and we have battled mightily to hold on to our faith. When others have left, Nate has stayed. He is a dear friend and a spiritual guide. I am so blessed to minister alongside him. Almost every week at Sandals Church, as I preach a message that God has laid on my heart, Nate sits in the studio recording. He senses what the Spirit is saying to the thousands of people who meet in community groups to discuss the sermon, what God is saying to our Church as a whole, and to each individual. Nate then writes the discussion guide and questions that our groups follow. Nate has this role because I trust him, and you can too. If this book had been available to me when I started Sandals Church many years ago, I would have avoided a multitude of pitfalls. Nate shares his wisdom and biblical insights to help you gain yours.

Nate is gifted at helping people connect with God, and it is my honor to recommend this beautiful work to bless your spiritual life in Christ. Nate has created a road map to deepen your relationship with God and to heighten your awareness of things that God is calling you to remove that have created obstacles in your relationship with Him. I pray that you will not only know the narrow road but learn to stay on it and grow in Christ from its many challenges.

Pastor Matthew Stephen Brown
Sandals Church

INTRODUCTION

Do you ever find yourself feeling like God is distant?

Maybe this distance is something that you have somehow instigated, knowingly or not. Distance from God is often the subject of many a Sunday sermon, teaching us how to identify our sinful patterns, how to repent of these, and how to then live a good life that hopefully has some meaning and a nice little ticket to heaven at the end.

Maybe something deep inside tells you that there is more to be had from the Christian life. Maybe you've been doing all the right things (at least as best as you know how), genuinely trying in earnest to pursue God and yet find that He still feels distant, despite your sincere efforts.

Maybe you read stories in the Bible about God intimately interacting with His people and you believe that those stories are from sometime in the distant past and not for our time. For if they were relevant to today, you would certainly be feeling His presence in your life–you would have stories to share of Him speaking to you, guiding you, showing you His love.

Maybe those times have been few and far between, if at all.

The Bible tells us that a name for Jesus is Emmanuel, which literally means, "God with us".

So why do we tend to live our lives like God is somewhere "up there" instead? If God is truly with us, why do we perceive Him as distant? Mostly benevolent perhaps, but also a bit detached, like someone tuning into the reality show of our lives. Sure, He is rooting for us and yes, He has the benefit of a broader perspective, but at the end of the day, God seems distant, detached, and has very little to do with our daily lives.

Think about the consequences of this mindset.

When we view God this way, we can find ourselves feeling alone and apart from this distant God who rules over the big stuff of the universe but doesn't really have a vested involvement in our lives. We may then find ourselves prone to living in fear, wondering when the other shoe is going to drop, especially when things feel like they're going well–a detached God, of course, would barely even know that good things were happening in our lives, or that bad things might be just around the corner.

We live life looking over our shoulders, wondering what could be lurking in the shadows of our lives, ready to pounce on us at any given moment.

We find ourselves guarded in our relationships, in our decisions, and in our workplaces because at our core we feel alone and that others cannot be trusted.

But what if that could change?

What could our lives look like if Jesus were literally walking beside us, sitting in the office with us, gathering around family dinners with us? Watching our favorite shows with us?

I don't read any story in scripture that seems to indicate that those who got to experience Jesus in person had any feelings other than peace, significance, belonging, and being known.

Aren't these the very things our souls crave?

Aren't these the very things we seek after, hoping to find peace in our surroundings, significance in our work, a sense of belonging in our relationships? Why else do we see so many people moving to a different state, switching jobs, posting desperately and endlessly on their social media accounts eager for that "thumbs up" or praise in the comment section?

Aren't all these somehow tied into a desperate sense of wanting to be *known*? If we were known on a deep, soul-level, we might be more content living where we are–for we would understand that external peace is fleeting, whereas inner peace is sustainable. We would be less prone to seek significance from our careers because we would know deep inside that as image-bearers, we carry unmatched significance. We wouldn't feel the need to check the status of our latest post, seeking the affirmation of others, because we would know that the Creator of the universe delights in us more than anyone else possibly could.

Being known is what our souls are after, and being known by God is the only thing that truly sustains.

I ask you to consider: How might our souls be different if we truly believed that God was right here, *with us*, right now? Not *up there*, but right beside us?

I imagine, like the gentlemen on the road to Emmaus, our hearts would burn within us, because at our core, we would feel the most intimate connection with the One who created our very souls. Our hearts would burn because we would feel *known, loved,* and *seen.* And if we knew, beyond a shadow of a doubt, that we were known, loved, and seen, I believe our lives would look quite different than they do right now.

When faced with setbacks, we might navigate them more easily because we would know that God is walking through those setbacks with us and that His very presence would provide peace amid the uncertainty.

We would navigate our relationships more securely, knowing that only through vulnerability can true relational intimacy be found.

We would navigate our workplaces more confidently, knowing that God has equipped us to do good work and that His guidance will be sufficient for any given day.

When we view God as *out there,* we rob ourselves of the full life that Jesus promised. It could be argued that seeing God as *out there* might actually be a form of denying Jesus. Denying the very Emmanuel who came to save our souls.

If you are looking for a life that stands out as different from the world around you, if you are looking for peace deep inside, if you could use a little dose of significance, if you desperately are seeking belonging, then this book is for you.

The secret to experiencing those things is actually much closer than we might think. I believe it is right here, *with us,* right now and all the time.

The secret is learning how to walk with Emmanuel.

Not getting ahead of Him, not putting Him high on a shelf, not forgetting Him, but walking with Him in our current circumstances and our current moment in time. Because to walk with Jesus is to commune with Jesus. And as His disciples experienced, to commune with Jesus is to experience the fullness of life He promised.

This will require effort, because anything worthwhile on this planet requires effort. There will be resistance, because the Enemy of our souls wants nothing more than for them to be disconnected with God. There will be days where you feel connected, and others where you feel like God is distant.

This is all part of the process. This is what living a life of intentional communion with Jesus is all about.

Nobody expects you to get it perfectly, ever. But I do pray that as you put into practice the ideas in this book, you will be blessed with more and more of Jesus, and that the blessing will translate into unmatched peace, a deep sense of belonging, and a daily communion with God that gives your life such significance and meaning that you can't help but share that significance with others.

Here's to the journey …

PART ONE
THE PATH

CHAPTER 1

THUNDER IN THE DESERT: PREPARE THE WAY FOR THE LORD (PART 1)

When Jews from Jerusalem sent a group of priests and officials to ask John who he was, he was completely honest. He didn't evade the question. He told the plain truth: "I am not the Messiah."

They pressed him, "Who, then? Elijah?"

"I am not."

"The Prophet?"

"No."

Exasperated, they said, "Who, then? We need an answer for those who sent us. Tell us something—anything!—about yourself."

"I'm thunder in the desert: 'Make the road straight for God!' I'm doing what the prophet Isaiah preached."

—John 1:19–24 (MSG)

When John the Baptist entered the scene in Israel, he came off as a bit of a madman eating locusts and wearing animal skins for clothing. Talk about making a memorable entrance for your career. If John were on Instagram today, something tells me that video would go viral in a heartbeat. I mean, of all the strange things we see on the internet, I'm not sure much would compare with an animal-skin-wearing, locust-eating, hairy guy roaming the barren desert. That dude sitting with his feet up in the Capitol building on January 6 would have nothing on John the Baptist.

Eccentric though he was, his self-proclaimed and primary mission was to get people to prepare their hearts for the coming of Jesus. His message was simple; quoting the prophet Isaiah, he simply wanted people to straighten their paths to make way for the coming Messiah.

This coming Messiah would be the salvation of the world, reuniting people's hearts with the Creator of the universe, bringing back a restoration of Eden's connection between God and humankind, restoring the intimacy of those evening walks in the garden, sharing in life's moments together. He would bring about hope and peace and give an opportunity for the entirety of humanity to experience the unending love of God. He would start by resuming those evening walks, thousands of years after the Garden, with His chosen twelve from the people of Israel.

Clearly, something worked in John's message of preparing hearts, as we're all here today still pondering the thoughts, actions, and sayings of Jesus.

By all measurable standards, the plan was a success.

If you're like me, this all sounds great. I can appreciate how Israel must have felt, after centuries of oppression and silence from God, when a messenger came to them proclaiming the coming Messiah, and how exciting it must have felt knowing that this Jesus would be walking beside them soon enough. Sometimes I wish I were born in that age so that I could hear Jesus' voice, feel His touch, and share the same air as Him.

But God's plan had me born in this age. And scripture tells us that there is something special in God's economy about being born in an age when we aren't able to see Jesus but we choose to believe anyway.[1]

So I take that promise from scripture in hope—hope that God has something special for us in this day and age, hope that there might be the restoration of that Eden-like intimacy available to us today, and hope that we can find that peace that comes from walking with Jesus at our side.

So how do we get there?

The answer to that question has been echoing through the desert since John the Baptist shouted it all those years ago. The secret lies in the message of Isaiah 40, the scripture that John quoted from those dry and dusty hills:

> Prepare the way. Make the path straight.

What if John's admonition wasn't *just* about Jesus' coming way back then? *What if it were still applicable to our lives today?*

Let that idea sit for a minute. What if John's announcement of the coming Messiah was also just as true for us today?

And I'm not talking about simply the Messiah who we profess our faith in for that highly desired ticket to heaven. I'm talking about the Messiah who not only offers us heaven but who also healed the sick, comforted the poor, and brought hope to the desperate. The Messiah who saw Nathanael sitting under the oak tree and called

---

[1] See John 20:29.

Zacchaeus down from the sycamore and invited Himself over to his place for dinner.

What would our lives—and more importantly, our hearts—look like if we were able to experience these types of interactions with Jesus today? If we imagine that for a minute, we could anticipate all kinds of wonderful things, such as healing, fullness, and being known and seen on a heart level.

I believe that all of those things that Jesus did for his people back then, He wants to do right now. Our problem is that we don't truly believe that this is possible. Our problem is that our paths aren't straight; we aren't taking John the Baptist seriously.

If Jesus were to walk among us once again, it would be a revival of biblical proportions. We know from scripture that this won't happen until His triumphant return,[2] but if we allow ourselves to imagine just a bit, what could our world look like if He were to walk among us right now?

Imagine what our cities would look like.

Imagine what our schools would look like.

Imagine what our political systems would look like.

Imagine what our hearts would feel like.

I believe all of these are actually Jesus' plan announced through John all those years ago. I believe that with a bit of work, we can truly experience Emmanuel walking with us in our cities, schools, and political systems. But it starts with us; it starts with our hearts. We

---

[2] See Revelation 19.

have to prepare the way, and we have to be willing to do the work to make the path smooth.

My hope is that we will see that this is attainable and it will be some of the best "life work" you do. My hope is that it will yield all the peace and fullness your heart craves, for as it engages with its Creator, it can't help but be filled with life, hope, goodness, and sweetness.

Now let me say a couple words of caution.

First, while the contents of this book may seem prescriptive, nothing Jesus ever did was entirely prescriptive. Everything He did was *personal.* But like eating, sleeping, praying, and making regular time with God, those prescriptive things take on a personal nature as we practice them.

Second, our life experiences shape the way we view God. This is a huge point that cannot be taken lightly. The degree to which you have experienced difficulties, setbacks, or trauma will affect the way you see and experience God; someone who has had multiple traumatic experiences will see God with a very different lens than someone whose life has been relatively easy.

When you consider your life experiences, *please don't let the low moments color the truth about how much God dearly loves you. When we doubt His love for us, the Enemy gains ground over our hearts and the bad guys win. This is such a critical point here.*

I am in no way wanting to trivialize what your experiences have been. If you haven't had the chance to process these with a good Christian therapist, you really should consider seeking a trained professional. Almost all the people I know—at least the healthy ones—have gone to counseling to process their life's painful experiences. I feel that good counselors are an integral part in helping clear the path for God to do His most amazing work, so please consider professional help so you can process these things. We all have things we need to process, and those who say they are strong enough to process trauma on their own are likely either lying to themselves or have buried the hurt so far beneath the surface that it's probably at an unhealthy level.

So what I mean by *not letting the bad guys win* is this: If we let our pain overwrite our experience of God to the point that it has more influence and power than He does, then the pain wins. We need to create intentional space to process that pain so that the bad guys—or girls, bosses, parents, friends, or spouses—don't get the last word. Jesus' blood on the cross gets the last word (more on that in chapter 5), and His word for you is *good*.

OK, now that that's off my chest, let's start this process of clearing the path for God. To get there, we're going to take a deep dive into Isaiah 40. If it helped direct John the Baptist, then let's give it a shot at guiding us.

I've chosen The Message for my translation because honestly it rocks.[3]

You ready?

Let's roll up our sleeves and dive into Isaiah 40 together.

---

[3] For a full confession, I used to make fun of The Message, until I started reading it. It's just a really solid translation that speaks truth. If you don't like The Message, please don't throw out my message; just swap my preferred version for yours, and I'm pretty sure we'll all still be friends at the end of the day.

CHAPTER 2

THUNDER IN THE DESERT: PREPARE THE WAY FOR THE LORD (PART 2)

"Comfort, oh comfort my people,"
says your God.
"Speak softly and tenderly to Jerusalem,
but also make it very clear
That she has served her sentence,
that her sin is taken care of—forgiven!
She's been punished enough and more than enough,
and now it's over and done with."

Thunder in the desert!
"Prepare for God's arrival!
Make the road straight and smooth,
a highway fit for our God.
Fill in the valleys,
level off the hills,
Smooth out the ruts,
clear out the rocks.

> Then God's bright glory will shine
> and everyone will see it.
> Yes. Just as God has said."
>
> —Isaiah 40:1–5 (MSG)

My wife and I have three teenage boys living in our house. I know what you're thinking–pray for those two, especially for their finances, because with three teenage boys sharing the same kitchen, I don't think there are enough Costco runs available to keep those strapping lads aptly-fed. When we talk about the spiritual concept of *surrender* in our household, it can often be misinterpreted as referring to who gets the last serving of pasta and meatballs.

Two of them are in high school and we're fortunate to live close enough to where the school is a three-minute drive. We live in Southern California. People drive everywhere; to walk anywhere but your mailbox is simply not done around these parts. I even know people who stop at the mailbox en route before completing their not-so-long drive up the driveway. It's just a thing we do out here, probably because we'd rather experience the great weather in limited quantities, to keep the rest of the country from being too jealous, and so we stay insulated from it in our cars, homes, and workplaces.

But I digress.

A few months ago, my boys' high school embarked on a project to transform its football field from grass to turf (another thing we do out here–some call it water conservation, critics call it a love affair with all that is fake), as well as upgrading the track from dirt to a composite material.

In my simplistic understanding of construction projects, this should be a relatively easy endeavor. Pull out the grass, do a quick leveling-off of the damage you've created by pulling out said grass, maybe rake the dirt on the track, put down the new materials, and *voila!* New track and field. I'm guessing this approach might be why they didn't hire me to do the job, although I'm pretty sure I would have at least had the project wrapped up a long time ago.

I would imagine there are a lot of us out there who take a similar approach to our spiritual lives.

Whether due to simple naivete, impatience, or an overly simplistic approach to our walk with God, many of us take the "quick fix" approach to our faith journeys.

I'm not saying this to heap shame on anyone. Remember, I would have gone for the quick fix with the track and field myself. But I do want to point out that maybe there is more involved in the process that we should consider.

In a world of rapid solutions, streaming video, and endless info on demand, there are still some areas of life that are subject to a different set of rules–rules where you can't skip steps, and you just have to do things the right, slow, and thorough way.

I think of construction and farming as two great examples; no matter how much technology advances, no matter how efficient new tools make those jobs easier, there are still some things about both lines of work that you just cannot create shortcuts for.

So, back to the track and field:

It has been months since they've started this project. I drive by the school every day, and I see tractors moving, workers working, and progress being made. Well, let me clarify that last one: I *trust* that progress is being made.

The demolition was quite quick. I think they had that part nailed within a couple of days. But then, over the next several months, I've seen dirt piles created, moved, and moved again.

Every time I drive by, I notice rocks. Lots of them. Big rocks, small rocks, medium-sized rocks, all piled up along the perimeter of the project. And every time I drive by, I think to myself: *I'm so glad there's someone leading that project who knows what they're doing.* Because I would never have thought so much would need to be done beneath the surface for such a "simple" project. I would never have guessed that there was such a need for being so thorough.

I have no idea whether John the Baptist had any construction experience, but his message was on point when it comes to how we should be approaching the task of preparing our hearts for Jesus.

First, let me preface by saying that this all comes in the context of *comfort* (verse 1). As Jesus said, His burden is light and His yoke is easy[1]. I think we sometimes misunderstand this saying to mean that we don't really have to do much or try too hard to access the love of Jesus. While there may be some truth in that—at least on a surface level—those who experience the kingdom in its fullness all end up having work to do. Think of the parables Jesus taught: There are farmers plowing fields, workers gathering the harvest, and people selling possessions to purchase a field.

This concept stands in stark contrast to one of the biggest lies of our current age–that we don't have to work at things to see results. That simply isn't true, and when Jesus says His yoke is easy, He is still communicating that we have to carry *something*. He just means that while we're working, we'll experience the "lightness" of having work that actually frees us rather than burdens us.

---

[1] See Matthew 11:28–30.

So in the context of receiving comfort, we are given a few things to consider in order to have the most fulfilling, life-giving journey with Jesus:

We need to make the road straight and smooth.

We need to fill in the valleys.

We need to level off the hills, smooth out the ruts, and clear out the rocks.

This "preparation work" comes with a promise: *"Then God's bright glory will shine, and everyone will see it.[2]"*

Whenever God's glory shone through His people, it was a source of awe and wonder to those who observed it, but imagine how it felt for the person whose face was shining? Think about Moses as he came down from Sinai–his face shone so bright that he had to cover it[3]. Why? Because he had a personal encounter with God Himself. The implication is that the closer we get to God, the more we reflect His characteristics; the more we reflect His glory. And since God is the source of all comfort, joy, peace, and security, we can assume that if we were to shine bright like the scripture says, we would by extension feel these same characteristics.

Sign me up for that.

Who of us couldn't benefit from more joy, more peace, and more security? Not only would we experience these things as a direct result of our communion with Jesus, but others would see it and hopefully be attracted to it.

---

[2] Isaiah 40:5.
[3] See Exodus 34:29–35.

Imagine if the reputation Christians had in the world today was that we shined so bright as people, that instead of others throwing shade on us, they had to wear shades[4]?

Let's begin doing the work by letting our imaginations carry out a little exercise for a minute. Don't worry—we're going to get to the heavy lifting soon, but I want to paint a little picture for you first.

Here's what I want you to picture:

Imagine some remote place out in the desert. Your view is big, and you see mountains off in the distance. Maybe it's sunset, and you can see the texture of purple hills and layers of rising mountains far off on the horizon.

Allow yourself to go there now. Imagine that you are standing on a wide, freshly paved road with absolutely no cars on it. The road is stretching out before you—a perfectly paved, smooth road going for miles—maybe it has a gentle rise off in the distance, followed by an easy turn as it approaches the base of faraway mountains.

Can you picture it?

What color is the sky in your image?

What is the temperature outside?

Now imagine a comforting breeze brush against your face. What temperature is the wind? What do you hear?

---

[4] OK, full confession: I borrowed that saying from my sons. For those who need a quick translation, "throwing shade" means criticizing someone else, talking bad publicly about them, etc. Give me grace—I'm just trying to fit in here.

THUNDER IN THE DESERT: PREPARE THE WAY FOR THE LORD (PART 2)

Are there birds soaring gently above?

Sit with this image for a bit. Allow it to take root in your memory, because we're going to refer back to it from time to time.

As you allow your imagination to continue to paint this picture, notice the places in the road where the hills have been leveled off. Pay attention to those other places where small valleys have been filled.

Perhaps you see rocks pushed off the road and onto the shoulder of the highway. Maybe you see some big ones, others that are medium-sized, and still others that are small.

Again, sit with this image for a bit.

What feelings come up for you as you imagine this?

Do you feel a sense of peace? Rest? Stillness? Perhaps you feel *shalom*?

(If you recall, the Hebrew word 'shalom' refers to the feeling of deep, inner, and complete peace and fullness that comes from resting in the presence of God.)

Now allow yourself to picture that highway as a metaphor for your heart. As you picture it freshly paved, smooth, wide, and clutter-free, imagine that this represents your accessibility to communion with God[5].

---

[5] I know that from a theological perspective, God moves towards us without regard to the obstacles in His path. While I'm not trying to make a case against that notion that God pursues us, I am trying to argue that we have a role to play in making things easier—and that through clearing the path, we remove unnecessary pain, obstacles, hindrances that would stand in our way of understanding and experiencing the fullness of God that Jesus promised in John 10:10.

CLEARING THE PATH

Imagine that road as a pathway to your heart–a heart that is "prepared for the coming of the Lord". Picture how traveling down that road would be something that would happen with ease.

Why?

Because the preparation work had been done. The hills that stood in the way of the road were leveled. The valleys that caused unnecessary dips were filled in. The rocks cluttering the path were removed. The ruts were filled.

And with this well-prepared road stretching off into the distance, we have created a space for Jesus—for Emmanuel—to walk alongside us, to minister to us, to allow our hearts to "burn within" just like the fellas who walked to Emmaus with Him[6].

OK–so you're probably thinking to yourself: *This sounds great, and I'm following you with the metaphor, but how does this actually play out in my heart? What do you mean by hills, valleys, ruts, and boulders?*

Let's consider these from a big-picture perspective before we dig deeper later in the book.

What if the valleys represented those areas of emptiness that we feel–voids that we either ignore or try to numb by things that aren't from God?

The goal would be to fill the voids with spiritually healthy things.

What if the hills represented the big things that need to be removed from our hearts and minds? Those large obstacles that stand in the way of you and God, making access incredibly difficult.

---

[6] Luke 24:13–35.

The goal would be to remove the hills.

And what if the ruts represented the habits and practices that either bring us closer to God or move us subtly further away from Him? More on this in chapter 5, but a diligent practice of "filling in the ruts" will make a world of difference in your life.

Finally, what if the rocks represented all those other things that hinder our communion with Jesus? These are often the most difficult to identify but can yield incredible results such as joy, peace, and shalom when we deal with them.

The goal would be to remove the rocks that clutter our lives so we could have regular communion with Emmanuel.

Now, let's assume we accomplish all the above, and practice operating from that place of deep communion with God. This communion will actually help inform us of our truest identity—an identity rooted in truth and in stability rather than in our own questions and feelings. In our current world where identity is king and God is nowhere in the picture, what could our lives look like if we put God as King and then let Him speak to our identity?

Imagine operating out a sense of this deep security in who God has made you to be. How much of a life-giving difference would that make? We would more closely reflect the life of Jesus–living His life of peace, significance, and deep connection with the Father.

The aim of this book is to help usher God's presence into our lives, allowing Him to remind us of our identity as His beloved sons and daughters so that out of that place we can live lives that are truly God-glorifying. Lives that are a calm, stable force in a world that is sadly, anything but calm and stable.

This entire process starts by first *identifying* what clutters our lives, hindering our communion with Jesus, and then *doing the work* to deal with them.

For now, let's simply ask Jesus for help in identifying these. As God begins to reveal these areas, I would strongly encourage you to keep a journal. Consider breaking these into four sections: Valleys, Hills, Ruts, and Rocks. We'll define each of these in the coming chapters, but allocating separate sections of your journal will prove fruitful here.

Let's pray this together:

> *Father, Jesus, Holy Spirit, my soul longs for communion with You. I confess all the areas where my heart goes searching for You that are not from You. I confess that I am weak, prone to wander, and yet at the same time I deeply desire Your love and Your presence.*
>
> *Help me with the process of identifying the valleys, hills, ruts, and rocks in my life. There are some that I can easily identify, and there are others that I will need Your grace to reveal.*
>
> *I open myself up to this process, Lord, and I ask You to deal gently with me as I seek to clear the path of my heart for You.*
>
> *I trust You, Lord, and look with eager expectation for the work You will do in my heart through this process.*
>
> *In Jesus' name, amen.*

CHAPTER 3

FILL THOSE VALLEYS

So Jesus left the Judean countryside and went back to Galilee.

To get there, he had to pass through Samaria. He came into Sychar, a Samaritan village that bordered the field Jacob had given his son Joseph. Jacob's well was still there. Jesus, worn out by the trip, sat down at the well. It was noon.

A woman, a Samaritan, came to draw water. Jesus said, "Would you give me a drink of water?" (His disciples had gone to the village to buy food for lunch.)

The Samaritan woman, taken aback, asked, "How come you, a Jew, are asking me, a Samaritan woman, for a drink?" (Jews in those days wouldn't be caught dead talking to Samaritans.)

Jesus answered, "If you knew the generosity of God and who I am, you would be asking me for a drink, and I would give you fresh, living water."

The woman said, "Sir, you don't even have a bucket to draw with, and this well is deep. So how are you going to get this 'living water'? Are you a better man than our ancestor Jacob, who dug this well and drank from it, he and his sons and livestock, and passed it down to us?"

Jesus said, "Everyone who drinks this water will get thirsty again and again. Anyone who drinks the water I give will never thirst—not ever. The water I give will be an artesian spring within, gushing fountains of endless life."

The woman said, "Sir, give me this water so I won't ever get thirsty, won't ever have to come back to this well again!"

He said, "Go call your husband and then come back."

"I have no husband," she said.

"That's nicely put: 'I have no husband.' You've had five husbands, and the man you're living with now isn't even your husband. You spoke the truth there, sure enough."

—John 4:3b–18 (MSG)

When I was in high school and first heard this passage, the teenage boy in me was proud of Jesus. Proud of the way He "laid the smackdown" (as we would say) on the Samaritan woman, calling her out for having multiple husbands and then not even bothering to get married to the man she was currently with. If I had been there and had been watching Jesus go to work, I would have wanted to give Him a high five.

Looking at this passage as an adult, I think if teenage me had been there sticking my hand out for a high five, I wonder if Jesus might have been tempted to throw me down the well.

FILL THOSE VALLEYS

At a minimum, I imagine Jesus would have encouraged me to pump the brakes a bit and would have gently reminded me that I was missing the point, big-time.

The point of this story is not that Jesus put this woman in her place.

Well actually it is, but not in the way you might you think.

For a woman of that time period to have had multiple husbands would have meant that she had been rejected by them. Again and again. Rejected to the point that she had basically given up on marriage altogether, playing it safe with dude number six, forgoing the "tying of the knot" because when one has been cast aside time and time again, the normal formalities lose their sense of hope and of meaning.

One of the things Jesus is doing here is pointing out the void in her heart that she has been trying to fill with men. A void that makes a lot of sense. I imagine a big part of her carried the lingering questions of *am I seen? Am I lovable? Does anyone even care about me?*

In one brilliant move, Jesus answers a resounding *YES!* to all of her questions.

And that "yes" meant so much to her that she grabbed her fellow villagers, who then persuaded Jesus to stay for another two days, because whatever it was Jesus offered, it *filled them* on a level they had never been filled before.

We could talk for hours about this amazing scene and the many intricacies here, but for now I just want to offer the following for consideration:

Jesus, in His brilliance, offers "living water"–something that never runs out. It does not disappoint and does not leave us feeling empty.

CLEARING THE PATH

Jesus offers a filling of the voids in our hearts.

How many times have you been disappointed with life?

How many times have you felt like you needed to hide from others, going about your business in intentional anonymity?

How often have you gone to *that well*, only to end up thirsty again?

Whether or not you've had five husbands, I think on a heart-level we can all find a little in common with this woman.

So from the perspective of a teenage boy, Jesus puts the woman in her place, which He certainly does, but in the typical unexpected way Jesus operates:

He says her place is right there, with Him, receiving His love and His acceptance into the eternal kingdom of God *(which is not referring to a "future place", but rather something infinite, which also includes the here and now).*

Her place includes (and perhaps is predicated on) Jesus filling the voids in her heart—voids where she has sought the answers to her deep questions by men, but who keep leaving her feeling empty and unseen.

So the big question is, what are the voids in your heart that you are filling with things other than Jesus?

Now, hear my heart here: This is not a question intended to make you feel any sense of shame but rather an honest question intended to bring to light any areas where you may find yourself bringing your big questions—those areas that could really benefit from hearing the powerful voice of Jesus, and not the powerless voices of substitutes.

When you consider your own personal voids, know that we all run to fill the voids. It's one of the reasons why smartphones are so prevalent in our society today. It's one of the reasons the entertainment industry is so successful. It's one of the reasons why pornography will never go away.

These industries are all so successful because they have been built on our collective voids, capitalizing on our felt need to fill the emptiness with something—with *anything*, even if the satisfaction is fleeting.

FILLING THE VALLEYS

> Thunder in the desert!
> "Prepare for God's arrival!
> Make the road straight and smooth,
> a highway fit for our God.
> Fill in the valleys,
> level off the hills,
> Smooth out the ruts,
> clear out the rocks.
> Then God's bright glory will shine
> and everyone will see it.
> Yes. Just as God has said."
>
> —Isaiah 40:3–5 (MSG)

The first thing Isaiah recommends for preparing our hearts for Jesus is that we fill in the valleys.

He's referring to those places in our lives that feel empty and lacking– the voids, if you will.

But the caveat is that we must fill them with the right things. And if you look around at culture (pick any time in human history), we, like the woman at the well, are masters at filling the voids with water that makes us thirsty again and again.

It's why the woman at the well was so interested in the water that Jesus offered.

It's the same reason why we, as a Western society, self-medicate on so many levels.

If you need convincing, start by examining what you do when you are bored. And I'm not talking about the *I've got absolutely nothing to do so let me fill up the hours* type of boredom, I'm talking about the *I've got precious seconds that aren't currently filled up* level of boredom.

You're filling up the gas in your car, and you have a minute and a half to kill.

You're standing in line at the grocery store and you've got nothing to do.

You're early to an appointment so you've got ten minutes before your meeting starts.

What do you do?

I'm not much of a betting man, but if I were, I would lay down some serious cash that you are on your phone in some capacity. Maybe playing a game, catching up on Instagram, knocking out a few emails, or checking the news.

But you're on your phone.

Why?

Silence often brings up all kinds of things that we find deeply unsettling, so we anesthetize those difficult emotions by hiding from them in distractions and busyness.

Don't believe me? Try *not* pulling out your phone next time you find yourself in one of the aforementioned situations and see what surfaces.

I'm not trying to harp on smartphones here (although they are such an easy target); I'm simply wanting to point out that we all have voids in our lives. If we pay attention to it, boredom can serve a wonderful purpose of shining a light on where we run to fill that void.

And Isaiah suggests we do something about it.

THE INNOCUOUS FILLERS

Much of what I stated above would be considered pretty harmless. I know, an argument could be made (and I've made it thousands of times myself at the dinner table with my teenage boys) that constantly being addicted to our smartphones is quite unhealthy. And I do think it is unhealthy.

But by *harmless* in this context, I'm referring to those things that don't really have a major impact on our morality, on our good standing with others, or anything with any legal ramifications. Being on your phone isn't inherently a bad thing. Social media isn't necessarily a bad thing. Nor is the news, nor is sending work emails, playing games, or any other thing we do to pass the time. I'm not here to argue that they are bad things. They are merely *things*.

My question is, are they fruitful things?

Are we turning to these distractions to fill something in our life that we perhaps might even be blind to?

~~~~

When the kids were little, we used to practice a weekly technology Sabbath.

We wanted our kids to learn what it was like to not have screens at the ready at any and all times they desired. We did a technology Sabbath because as a married couple, we also needed time together where we weren't glued to our phones, or on-call for text messages or emails.

And if I'm honest, I'll offer two confessions:

First, I mention this Sabbath thing in the past tense, because when teenage boys go hang out with friends, you want your phone nearby in case something comes up. When your kids play club soccer, you need your phone for navigation, team communication, and let's face it, the ability to find the best-reviewed lunch spot in town so you can be known as the team foodie.

So we've had to practice Sabbath in other ways, and to be candid, I can tell when we're not doing a great job of it; my body and my spirit let me know pretty quickly.

And encouraging your teenagers to do the same is even more difficult, so pray for us—we could use it.

The second confession is that our technology Sabbath was *really difficult*. Not because turning our phones off was technically challenging, but because it was emotionally torturous, at least at first. I would notice all kinds of things come up for me, emerging from some hidden depth that I didn't even know existed. The magnetic pull to "just check my phone" happened literally hundreds of times each day. The not-so-subtle glancing at the clock, wondering how much more time until Sabbath was over, happened family-wide. In fact, as the clock would tick down, the boys would immediately rush to the television to turn on their favorite show, celebrating the end of Sabbath. (Yeah, we've already started saving up for their future therapy sessions.) When I was absent from my phone I would find myself wondering what my friends were up to, or what football games were on. In short, my mind was frantically trying to fill the space with all kinds of (arguably meaningless) activity.

Then, as the shock of 24 hours without technology started to wear off, bigger, deeper issues would surface:

Being in demand (as evidenced by emails, text messages, and the like) made me feel important, significant, and valued. Being bored made me feel exposed and vulnerable. Turning on my phone and finding that none of my friends had invited me to anything, made me feel unimportant and invisible.

Do you see the voids?

Those voids don't get exposed without some serious intentionality, often caused by withdrawing certain things from our lives for a short period of time. It's why the spiritual practices of Sabbath and fasting are so valuable (more on these in chapter 5).

The point here is merely to notice them. Write them down.

This process of noticing and writing is an integral part of filling the valleys; we have to be able to name what it is we're struggling against so we can begin the process of inviting God into those areas. Because like the woman at the well, the only way we're going to truly fill the voids is by allowing Jesus to speak directly into them.

So start by identifying them—that's the first step.

THE HARMFUL FILLERS

Now for a word on the other "void fillers".

While the fillers I mentioned above were relatively innocuous, there is another category that needs to be addressed–the self-destructive things we do to fill those really deep voids:

- Having been married to five men and living with the sixth.
- Requiring several alcoholic drinks when you get home from work.
- Being addicted to pornography.
- Texting that attractive coworker late at night while your spouse is asleep.
- Allowing your eyes (or your heart) to wander when you know it's not healthy.
- Being more and more comfortable bending the truth in order to protect your reputation.
- Living in a state of constant comparison—comparing your spouse, income, house, kids, or vacations to everything you see on social media and finding yourself increasingly discontented with the good things God has given you.

While these may appear to be major hills (sins) in our lives (which they are, of course), it is so incredibly helpful to view these as our own feeble attempts to fill the voids that lie deep within our hearts.

Without question, these need to be dealt with, because being an alcoholic or a porn addict or a habitual liar are dangerous—dangerous to yourself and dangerous to your relationships (both with God and with others).

FILL THOSE VALLEYS

As we work our way through this book, you will see that the valleys, hills, ruts, and rocks are all interrelated—as you deal with one area (a valley, for example) other areas will be addressed at the same time (perhaps exposing a hill), and they all lead to discovery (identification) and healing as we commit to the practices laid out in this book.

But a critical aspect of these "big-ticket" items is that they will destroy your relationships, finances, career, family, and many other good things in your life.

If you doubt me, take an honest read through the book of Proverbs and tell me that I'm wrong here.

So, rather than make you feel guilty for the way you fill the voids in your life, let's again start by simply identifying them. And I don't mean that the practice here is to say "I'm addicted to pornography or alcohol" (although naming it can often be the first step toward healing); I'm talking about the deeper-level stuff that is causing you to turn to pornography or alcohol in the first place.

A helpful process here is simply to name the destructive pattern and ask God to show you what it represents to you. Naming the pattern is good; understanding what drives that behavior, however, is where true healing is found. This healing comes from digging deep beneath the surface to reveal the voids that you are trying to fill through the destructive habits. And oftentimes, like the woman at the well, this practice requires the help of Jesus (or others who walk with Him and can help point these out to you).

Now, the reason I started with the "innocuous fillers" rather than the more obvious, harmful ones is that examining the harmless fillers will often point to the same heart-space that the bigger, more dangerous behaviors are trying to fill. So if you're having a hard time examining the heart-level issue that is at the root of you exploring an emotional relationship with someone other than your spouse, the first step is to stop the behavior, immediately.

If you struggle with drunkenness, make the decision to stop drinking excessively (maybe you need to make the decision to stop drinking anything at all, for a period of time while you gain control over the addiction). Remove the tempting apps on your phone that are causing you to stumble. Stop driving by that place that is the source of so much temptation. End the relationship with your coworker. Start telling the truth, no matter what.

We will take a much deeper dive into how to work through this in greater detail in the next chapter but for now, we deal with the problem by first stopping the behavior. Then, as the pull towards those things continues and you maintain the resolve to terminate these patterns, you look to name the voids you're trying to fill through these behaviors: removing the filler exposes the underlying void. Try practicing some of the tips laid out in the above section in order to help bring these to the surface:

- Try turning your phone off for 24 hours each week.
- Try not reaching for distractions when you find yourself with a few extra minutes of downtime in your day.
- Pay attention to what surfaces. Write these down.

Then, as God reveals these places in your heart, simply begin by inviting Him into that empty place. Pray something like this:

> *Jesus, I recognize that I am a broken individual, and that I have run to fill these empty places in my heart with things that are not of You. I choose now, in this moment, to reject the water that doesn't fill and that leaves me empty, and I instead choose Your living water.*

Fill me with this today, Jesus, for I need it.

I recognize that my heart has voids that can only be filled by You; come into these vulnerable places, Jesus, and fill me. Reveal anything here that You want to reveal, and may I be filled with the strength and courage to deal with these things today.

In Jesus' name, amen.

A WORD ABOUT VALLEYS—THEY START EASY

By their nature, valleys start off comfortable and easy.

I used to do a lot of cycling, and when I would be traveling along a road that had a large dip (or *valley*), it would offer such relief to coast on the downslope. It was a great time to catch my breath, relax, and let gravity take a turn in moving me along the road.

The problem was never the downhill. The problem was that whatever amount of elevation I lost coasting downhill, I then had to regain on the other end of the valley, and going uphill on a bike is really hard, slow, and can even be painful.

Sound familiar?

The peek on the website seems innocuous at first, but then it has a gravitational pull that sucks you further and further in.

The text message inviting you to lunch seems harmless, but then you both end up sharing emotional parts of your lives that probably shouldn't have been shared. But you feel safe there, and a connection is made, and now you're getting pulled downhill fast.

The after-work drink was no big deal, but now you can't function without it.

Going downhill is so easy.

The good news is that you have what it takes (provided you enlist the power and help of Jesus) to climb back up the other side of that valley. It will likely be difficult, it'll certainly be slow, and it may very well be painful, but it can be done. You just have to make the commitment to do it, to endure it, to keep fighting, and to enlist the help of other godly people.

SOME PRACTICAL WAYS TO CLIMB OUT

Think back to the very beginning of the lockdowns in 2020.

I heard story after story of how it was kind of nice, being asked to stay home. How the change of pace allowed for new richness in family time, how nice it was to not have to drive everywhere, and how there were such great shows on Netflix and Hulu. Our family enjoyed dinners on the patio, my wife and I enjoyed glasses of wine by the fire pit, and we all enjoyed taking a break from the frenetic pace of life in our day and age.

All of that happiness lasted about two weeks and then things started to shift. The isolation began to override our desire to be social. Watching church from the comfort of our couch, coffee in hand, pajamas still on, became an attractive solution to worshiping on the weekend even after in-person services had resumed. Spending time in digital meetings began to sell me on the benefits of not having to drive places to get things done. Shopping with Amazon and Instacart became such a convenience, so we stopped running by the local stores for our goods.

FILL THOSE VALLEYS

What started off as a nice respite from society quickly became a new habit; the downhill slope of being away from people began to gain momentum, and that momentum became really difficult to stop.

Here we are years later, and I still know people who have become so accustomed to isolation that they remain unwilling–or unable–to dig back out.

But as God said in the Garden, *it is not good for man to be alone*[1].

Please don't misunderstand me—I'm not harping on any of these in and of themselves. If you want the truth, I still do digital meetings, we almost always shop with Amazon and Instacart–these changes have afforded my life an increased measure of efficiency and convenience. The problem lies when we get sucked into the impersonal life rather than using those efficiencies to provide time for more in-person connection.

Climbing back up out of the valley, so to speak, starts with a recognition that God was on to something, even all those years ago.

Deep down, we all find it easier to isolate than to engage so when faced with the choice of engagement or efficiency, we often choose the latter.

I'm not saying this to make you feel guilty; I'm just as culpable as the next person, but I think it's worth noticing how often we make these types of choices.

And I'm not bashing efficiency, but it might prove helpful to pay attention to just how often "efficiency" removes "humanity" from our routines. As they say, knowing is half the battle. Maybe climbing out is the other half.

---

[1] See Genesis 2:18.

A few practical tips on how to climb out:

- Start small. Opt for shopping in person and choose to start a short conversation with the cashier.
- Instead of vegging out on the couch watching a show, consider playing a board game or engaging in simple conversation.
- Instead of hitting the drive-thru on your way home, swing by the market and pick up some artisan cheese and a baguette to snack on while you make a home-cooked meal with your family.

And like identifying the voids in our lives, begin to pay attention to what comes up for you as you practice these simple steps. How do you feel after playing the board game with your family? What is the condition of your heart after eating good food at a slower pace? How has the inclusion of others affected the way you feel at the end of your day?

Like the other feelings, write these down as well. The process of writing helps us access more of our heart, so it's well worth this extra step. All of these little processes can help facilitate the "climbing out" of the valleys.

NOW LET'S FILL THOSE VALLEYS

Now that we're on our way to the other side of these valleys, we need to fill them or we run the risk of falling back in. And recognizing that filling them with anything other than Jesus will ultimately leave us wanting, we need to be strategic with how we go about this. Since we were not meant to live alone, the first step in filling the valleys is that we absolutely *must* be intentional about engaging with Christian community. This starts by getting yourself back to church in person.

Now I know, many churches absolutely *killed it* with their online platforms over the past few years. I personally am a fan of how so many churches pivoted at a crucial time, putting out exceptional online content so that the gospel truly can be preached throughout the whole world. I support online church 100%. But I also think that watching church by yourself is no substitute for engaging in church with a community of believers. Even if that means gathering a few other friends and watching it–together–from your home.

Imagine if I showed you scenic pictures of the French alps. Imagine if I were an expert mountaineer and had traveled there extensively. I could walk you, step-by-step, through all of the mountain peaks, show you pictures of the local towns, pictures of the rivers, meadows, sunsets–everything.

And those images would likely stir you if I were to do so. And while viewing the pictures would be *good*, wouldn't being there be *so much better*? In a similar manner, a video of someone jumping off high rocks into a river with incredible scenery in the background is great, but jumping in yourself is the real deal.

Watching an online worship service is so much better than not watching one at all, but standing in a room full of other Jesus-followers, gathering in corporate worship and singing together, praying together, being in God's presence together–that is where it gets amazing. So please, like every other practice in this book, just try it for a few weeks. See what it does for your soul.

After you've spent some time in corporate worship, consider what it would look like to be a part of a smaller Christian community. Most churches have small groups that meet during the week; what would it look like to commit to joining one? Of course, it takes effort and commitment, but nobody said filling valleys was supposed to be a cakewalk.

One of the consistently richest parts of my week is when my wife and I host a small group at our house. It's a place for us (and others) to come together, to discuss what God is doing in our lives, pray for one another, and support each other. It helps fill a valley for me—specifically, the void that comes from me feeling like I'm all alone—and it gives me a space to both minister, and be ministered to, from other like-minded Jesus-followers.

Others I know are part of a men's or women's group, some volunteer with youth programs. The point is to get in community with other believers. As one person put it, you can neither love nor receive love if you're by yourself on an island. We need others around us.

So, *church*, and *church community*.

Commit to giving it a try for a few weeks. Don't be afraid to journal through the highs and the lows, the joys and the fears. In all of it, invite Jesus into the experience and pay attention to how He shows up for you.

I'm confident that He will, and I'm confident that in doing this, you will be well on your way to partnering with Jesus to fill the valleys along the path to your heart.

CHAPTER 4
BULLDOZE THOSE HILLS!

"Therefore, since we are surrounded by such a great cloud of witnesses, let us throw off everything that hinders and the sin that so easily entangles. And let us run with perseverance the race marked out for us"

—Hebrews 12:1 (NIV)

The track and field near my house is nowhere near done, yet I can't help but imagine what that space will look like when it's finished. What is currently a bunch of dirt and rock piles will eventually become a place where athletes train and compete, where students celebrate in victory, and where lots of hard work will either return a trophy or a sense of defeat and loss.

What's interesting about the track events that will be held there is that while track is mostly an individual sport, it is also a sport where the whole team rallies around its athletes, cheering them on when they do well. When an individual does well, his or her placement in the race impacts the entire team's standings in the overall competition. It's really a beautiful thing to know that your teammates are cheering you on as you push yourself toward the finish line.

I heard a sermon once that talked about track races—specifically the relay races during track meets.

Let's look at the 4x400 relay race. Four athletes each take a turn racing one lap around the track. The baton is passed, the next athlete takes their turn, races around the track, passes the baton, and so on.

What this preacher pointed out that was so incredibly profound was this: The first athlete does not run their lap, tell themself that their job is done, head for the showers, clean up, and head home.

No, they stay and cheer on the next runner. After the second runner is done, both runners now cheer on the next athlete on their team. After the third finishes, the whole relay team is now cheering on the final runner. None of the runners is alone in this type of race; they all have teammates who have a vested interest in them competing well and finishing strong.

Now imagine all the saints throughout human history.

Imagine *you* carrying a baton, running your race.

And while you may feel alone in your lane, and while nobody knows your unique struggles, regardless of what you yourself are experiencing uniquely, you are also being cheered on by all of the athletes (saints) who have gone before you.

Pause and sit with that concept for just a minute. *You are not alone.* You have generations of saints cheering you on, their support echoing throughout heaven's corridors. People are rooting for you; rooting for you to run well, to finish strong, and to keep enduring.

This is the *cloud of witnesses* the author of Hebrews is referring to. And what are they cheering for? They're cheering for you to throw off everything that hinders, and the sin that so easily entangles.

An athlete in a relay race clearly wouldn't run well if they were carrying the extra weight of a hiking backpack over their shoulders or if their legs were tangled up in rope.

Shed those things, however, and your strength will show and your "lightness" will give you new speed. Couple that with the support of generations of witnesses, and you've got yourself a race.

IDENTIFICATION

Let's begin the identification process by looking at entanglement.

It is these entanglements that I'm going to call the *hills* in our lives—those big things that stand in the way of our communion with God. The hills are usually pretty easy to identify. Start by simply asking yourself, *what do I know is wrong but I keep doing anyways?* You and I both could probably fill pages with this list, but let's start with the big stuff. In God's system, there is no sin that is too great for God to deal with. Let's all pause and say a huge *amen* to that. But sometimes people can take the approach that because we are saved by grace, we can keep on living our lives of sin.

The writer of Hebrews makes it pretty clear that this is not how it works–if we continue in our ways of sin, willingly defying God and His commandments, we are denying Christ and His sacrifice on the cross[1].

---

[1] See Hebrews 10:26–30.

Jesus paid a pretty high price so you and I could walk with Him throughout our lives. If we knowingly continue on a path that is in open defiance of what God says is best for us, we essentially are saying that the sacrifice of Jesus doesn't matter. This concept isn't coming from me, but from the apostle Paul himself, so if you want to send a hateful email, please address it to stpaul@heaven.org and I'm sure he'll be right in touch.

Now that that's off my chest, let's talk about how to deal with the hills. First, begin by identifying them. Write them down in your journal and be as specific as possible.

- *I need to stop viewing pornography.*
- *I drink too much alcohol on a regular basis.*
- *I need to move out of my boyfriend's house and stop sleeping with him.*
- *I need to end that inappropriate relationship.*
- *I let anger control me and it affects my relationships.*
- *I need to tell the truth even when it affects my reputation.*

It may be tempting to get more granular *(I have too much pride in my heart)*, and that's OK. Just know that for now, we want to focus on the big stuff; we'll get to the smaller things later, so write them down and just be willing to move them to a different category later down the road (see what I did there?)

Now, a quick word of caution: You might feel some things stirring in you as you populate your list. Please pay attention to whether you feel *convicted* or *accused*. The Holy Spirit will convict us but will never accuse us. *Accusation* tells us that we are worthless, unlovable, defective. *Conviction* tells us that we are not worthy (yet still have incredible worth), are loved deeply and are broken (but not defective). Accusation is from the Enemy; conviction is from the Spirit.

When you feel convicted simply give those things to God. Let Him know how bad you feel that this is a part of your life. Ask Him to free you of any sinful habits you might have so that their power is removed from your life[2]. Confession doesn't need to be a formal process or be done while sitting in a wooden box; it simply needs to be done out of a pure place in your heart.

A good picture of confession would be that of a child coming to his father, crying because he knew he did something wrong and feels terrible about it. And I know not everyone had a good father, but imagine if instead of erupting in outrage, the father holds his child, picks him up, and reassures him that he is still loved, still part of the family, and still accepted–even though the child did something wrong.

That Good Father will still consider what type of consequences need to be enacted, but the time for the consequences is later. In the moment of confession, simply allow yourself to receive a big warm hug from your Father in heaven who has been waiting for you to confess for quite some time now. You may have several things you need to confess. It's OK–God is patient and will love you through each of the things on your list.

As you confess these to God, imagine yourself out in that desert, identifying the hills that block the way of the road, and putting together a plan to bulldoze them so that they no longer exist. The identification is the first step toward healing. It's the acknowledgement that something is standing in the way of you being filled with the fullness of God. It's making a plan to rid your life of these because you finally see the value in doing so.

---

[2] More on this in a bit, as I recognize that many of us who struggle with addictions would be quite satisfied with a simple prayer asking God to remove them; if that were the case, we wouldn't still be struggling. I get it. Stick with me–we'll take a deeper dive shortly.

Because let's face it—we only do the things we're motivated to do. And we're only motivated when we see the value. If I go to the doctor and she tells me I need to lose weight, that's the identification. That's a good thing. Now I know I need to do the work to shed a few pounds. But I won't actually make a change unless I believe that what she's saying has value.

I heard someone once say that we only change when the pain of staying the same outweighs the pain required to change. So in our metaphor, we're talking about steep hills, possibly even vertical ones, that are impeding our path. And the reward of a smooth path is communion with the Creator of the universe. It is a reuniting of our souls with God; a heart-level return to Eden, if you will.

I know that might sound abstract, but isn't that what your heart is after anyways?

Think about it: Why do you do those things you do?

When we know something is wrong; when we know it is in direct opposition to what God says is best for human flourishing, why do we still go toward those same vices over and over again?

I believe it's because our hearts are searching for some things that only God can truly provide: Comfort. Belonging. Significance.

Maybe you go to your vices because you are running from pain, so you seek the temporary comfort of sex, alcohol, or truth-bending. Perhaps in running to these, you feel loved for who you are for the first time in your life, or maybe you feel justified in your anger because you don't feel like God is defending you, so you defend yourself. These all make sense.

We weren't made to live lives of pain, lives of being invisible or weighed down by others' expectations of us. We weren't made to live lives of being alone.

God said as much in the Garden. But just like Adam and Eve, we fall prey to the notion that as beings created in the image of God, we too can be just like Him, but we err by thinking we can take our destinies into our own hands. *How has that worked out for us?*

The problem is, we're *finite* in every imaginable way. And finite beings cannot ponder the totality of the infinite because the very nature of *infinite* is that there is always more.

In a way, this ought to bring us comfort, because our infinite God has infinite love, infinite patience, and infinite mysteries to explore. Our infinite God knows infinitely more than we do, sees infinitely more than we see—the real question is whether we actually live our lives in constant awareness of this fact. Because if we did, we would trust that His plan for human flourishing, as laid out in the Bible, would be worth pursuing. Because if God is good, then His plan is good, and if His plan is good, then it can be trusted. And if God's plan can be trusted, He will give us the strength and ability to follow it.

Even though it can be hard sometimes.

Even though we mess up.

Even though, as the old song goes, we are prone to wander …

Thank God for His infinite nature, His infinite goodness, and His infinite love.

So, back to the hills.

If I can trust that the doctor truly has my best interest in mind by telling me I need to lose weight, then a natural follow-up question might be to ask *how*?

So let's talk about how.

How do we bulldoze those hills?

The first step is *identifying* them. Good job. You've done the easy part. Now let's roll up our sleeves for the next step.

CONFESSION

The next step is *confession*—to God and to others.

I know, many of you just now had a minor heart palpitation at the latter statement. You might be thinking, *OK, I'm cool with confessing to God. He knows my sin anyways, so I'm down with that. I actually paused and did that a few pages ago, and while that took courage and my heart was racing, I actually felt better, so that was a bonus. But now that you are telling me I need to confess to a real person, I'm already on my way to the Goodwill bookstore to donate this book, because there's no way in the world that I'm going to confess to a real person.*

I know. Confession is scary. I hate it every single time I do it.

I mentioned earlier that confession doesn't need to happen in a wooden box. God hears, and you don't need to say a prescribed number of special prayers to absolve yourself.

That's not what I'm talking about. I'm talking about offering a genuine apology to God for the things we do that offend Him:

> If we confess our sins, he is faithful and just and will forgive us our sins and purify us from all unrighteousness.
>
> —1 John 1:9 (NIV)

Praise God for that fact, that if we confess, He forgives. We live in a world where forgiveness is not the norm—people harbor bitterness and resentment against each other all the time—but when we confess to God, our good standing is restored and our hearts are made pure. And there is no trace of bitterness or resentment in Him. What a relief.

When I talk about confession, there are actually two parts to this. The first part offers *forgiveness* and the second part offers *healing*.

Have you ever done anything in your past that, when you think about it, you still shudder? Perhaps you are older now, wiser, and you look back on that decision, or that action, or that heart-posture, and you can hardly believe that was you? Perhaps you occasionally run across someone from that season in your life, and your anxiety spikes just a bit, because maybe they *heard*, or maybe they talked with someone who thought they saw you *there, with them, doing that thing*. You cross paths with them, and you secretly hope they don't recognize you all those years later, especially now that you've got a family and a different set of friends, and *oh my, if these people find out about* that thing *back then, they'll never view me the same again?*

I'm guessing we all have a thing or two that we prefer stays in the dark, right?

So this is where the two aspects of confession are critical. We first absolutely need to have forgiveness from God. God brings everything out into the light, and so we have to bring our stuff out from the darkness and into the light so that the blood of Jesus can cover it and so that we can be *forgiven* and *purified*.

What an utter relief there is in those two words.

But let's say you've done these things already. You've confessed to God, but still your heart pounds when you consider the deeds of your past (or maybe they're still in the present)? It's because the second aspect of confession hasn't been accomplished yet. You've been *forgiven*, but you haven't yet been *healed* from it, and because you haven't been healed, shame rears its ugly head.

> Therefore confess your sins to each other and pray for each other so that you may be healed. The prayer of a righteous person is powerful and effective.
>
> —James 5:16 (NIV)

Read that again, slowly. I think this verse often gets overlooked, especially since the second half packs such a punch.

If you grew up in church like I did, we heard this second part quoted all the time: "The prayer of a righteous person is powerful and effective."

It was used as encouragement to both be righteous and to seek out righteous people to pray for us. I agree with both of these things, but there seems to be a tie-in between righteousness and the first part of this verse: confession to one another.

Confess your sins to each other, so you may be healed.

Ugh. No wonder we focus on the second part.

Confessing to God is hard enough, but when we confess to another person, (and the context is that this person *knows* you and is not hidden from you), that's next-level exposure. Confession is so vulnerable, it often feels like we're fully exposed, baring all, and nobody enjoys that.

As proud humans, we are so self-protective, so we often skip the "confession to others" piece.

But what if, by confessing to others, we actually receive the true healing that Jesus offers?

What if by admitting to a real human that we've done something wrong, that we don't have it all together, that we've royally messed up, we allow the Spirit to do His best work in us and through that other person?

Because if Jesus is truly Emmanuel, God-with-us, then maybe that person you're confessing to is actually going to be used as God's instrument to usher in a whole new wave of healing for you? When we look someone else in the eye and tell them we're a mess, we give them the opportunity to show the love of Jesus to us by offering grace, by offering compassion, and by offering love.[3]

When that person offers these things, shame flees. Shame tells you that there's something wrong with you, and that if people *just knew*, they would never love you, because you are, at your core, unlovable.

And the power of confession to another person is that you put yourself in the vulnerable position of receiving love *when you have done something unlovable*. When we receive love under these circumstances, the lies of shame wither away under the strong light of love.

---

[3] By all means, you need to confess to safe, godly people who are intentional about their apprenticeship to Jesus. So choose carefully, but still choose.

It takes tremendous courage to do this, but I've rarely seen an act of courage go unrewarded. I would encourage you to find a safe person (perhaps a pastor or your small group leader) and start small. Test the waters. Ask Jesus for the courage to confess and the wisdom to find the right person and see what results.

I predict you will feel lighter afterwards.

And since we've been talking about keeping a journal throughout this book, I would encourage you to take the time to reflect after you do this. Write it down (our brains process things differently when we are writing them down, so this extra step yields all kinds of amazing results).

CHANGE

Now that we've identified the hills, practiced confession to God and to others, we can now work on making changes to our lives. In church circles, we often refer to this as *repentance*, but I'm intentionally using the word *change* here instead. Repentance can sometimes take on an old feel to it, and often be wrongly interpreted to be an action that is isolated to our *intentions*, rather than the scope of our *entire actions*.

When Jesus told the woman caught in adultery to "go and sin no more", he didn't say "go and don't intend on sinning anymore". He simply said *don't*. He is referring to a life-change, not an intention-change.

So how do we truly change?

The secret to unlocking the power of change lies in the previous chapter: We start by identifying the voids in our hearts that we are trying to fill by something other than Jesus.

So take a minute and look back over your journal from the last chapter. What voids came to the surface as you intentionally removed distractions from your life?

Did you notice that you felt insignificant? Perhaps you felt unloved? Maybe you ran to escape, comfort, or pleasure as a means of avoiding some current discomfort or pain in your life? Or perhaps anxiety reared its ugly head as you realized you had far less control over the outcome of your life's events than you had previously thought?

Or—and this one has derailed humanity since that first bite of the fruit in the Garden—maybe you noticed that you don't really trust God's heart toward you[4]?

Certainly, many more "voids" can be listed here, but the idea is to pay attention to them, and to invite God into them. Once we've identified the infinite void we are trying to fill with finite measures, only then can we realize the necessity of bringing the Infinite into these specific areas.

When the woman caught in adultery was told by Jesus to go and sin no more, there is an assumption that He equipped her to do so.

Why?

I would imagine that it had something to do with Him revealing the void in her heart, speaking life into it, and then empowering her to really, actually change.

So here are a few tips that I think help to bring about real change.

---

[4] More on this shortly, I promise.

IT'S A HEART THING

Dallas Willard, the famous Christian philosopher, talked about the "gospel of sin management" in his epic work, The Divine Conspiracy. He observes how we, as Western Christians, can tend to run amok trying so hard to deal with the sin in our lives through methods that strictly focus on behavior.

If you've failed over and over again with a sin issue (a hill) in your life, you've likely failed because you were merely treating the symptoms and not the disease. If our objective is simply to "not sin", then we are on a failed mission.

So, when I talk about bulldozing the hills, I'm not saying the trick is simply to *try harder*, to apply incredible effort at not doing the things, and instead to just work really hard at pleasing God.

There is absolutely a place for self-control. Self-control gets us out of all kinds of trouble and is wholeheartedly necessary, but relying strictly on self-control to change your behavior is like a skydiver using his reserve parachute when jumping out of a plane without first trying his primary chute. The reserve parachute is for emergency purposes only—the main chute is the one that is designed to do the complete job. Self-control comes into play when your guard is down, when the Holy Spirit pings your radar to let you know that the path you're about to embark on is a dangerous one. Self-control gives us the power to make the decision to not travel down that road. It's a necessary muscle that absolutely must be exercised.[5]

---

[5] This is one of the reasons why the ancient practice of fasting is so helpful to our overall spiritual health. It exercises our "no" muscle and has immeasurable ripple effects for good. We'll dive into this more in chapter 6 but it is worth mentioning here.

But if we truly want to change, if we truly want to bulldoze the hills in our lives, we're going to need more than simply sin management. We're going to need to take a deep dive into what is going on at the heart level. Which is precisely why Isaiah recommends we start with the valleys; we start by paying attention to the voids that we're constantly trying to fill.

A technique that I've found incredibly helpful is this:

After I have identified the void (for this example, let's call it *significance*), when temptation presents itself, I then speak to that particular characteristic in my heart. If I'm struggling to feel significant and happen to notice an attractive woman at the gym, this triggers a tug-of-war in my heart. The sinful side of me (the writers in the New Testament would call this *the flesh*) wants to take a nice long look at the attractive female while I'm resting in-between sets. The spiritual side of me then tugs at me a different way, telling me to look elsewhere. Fill in the blanks with your own personal voids and temptations, and I'm certain you can relate.

I have found that the most success in winning this battle of the soul is when I pause and ask myself the following question: *what is my heart wanting to run to by looking at this woman?* Answer that question, and you've got yourself some genuine headway in winning the battle and in bulldozing that hill. I often pause and pray, asking God to reveal the answer to that question. Let's say the word *significance* pops up. I then tell myself: *She is not able to answer my heart's question on whether I am significant; only God can answer that question.*

Again, this prayer practice is a way of taking ground here in the battle.

Then I bring that question before God: *God, what do You say about my significance? Am I insignificant? Can You remind me of my significance in You right now, because my heart is feeling vulnerable and weak.*

Do you see how life-changing this approach is? Almost every time, God comes through in this type of prayer. And the times when it seems like He doesn't come through? That's when self-control takes over. That's when I either have to move to a different piece of exercise equipment or leave the gym altogether.

Some of you may be thinking that this sounds like pretty extreme behavior; it's just a woman, and you're just looking and not taking it any further. I would argue (from experience) that you are dead wrong there. When I indulge that behavior, I surrender a part of my heart to the finite. And the finite never satisfies but always ends up disappointing me and leaving me feeling empty over time.

When I recognize that the stakes are incredibly high, that there is a war for my very soul in that moment, and that I have access to the Infinite simply through a prayer, I can gain victory; I can bulldoze that hill. When I can do that, I then usher in all kinds of heart-healing from God Himself.

When I learn to take my "heart questions" to God and not to something else, I create space for Him to speak into those areas. This brings God's very breath of life back into my soul and in that moment, I am a little more like Adam in Eden, enjoying the company of a God who loves me enough to patiently work with me on the restoration of my soul back to Him.

Now, you and I both know that temptation is everywhere, and that we are incredibly forgetful creatures, especially when it comes to matters of the heart. If you've ever been to a Christian camp or retreat, you know exactly what I'm talking about. You come down the mountain on a spiritual high, only to be hit with reality days later. But if we keep in mind that this process is a heart thing, and not a behavior thing, we can then have the necessary tools to start making some real progress.

Keep in mind that bulldozing hills takes a lot of work, takes a lot of intentionality, and takes a ton of persistence.

So here is a list of questions I ask myself when I find I'm tempted to return to a sinful habit and as a result run the risk of rebuilding a hill:

- *What is my heart going after here?*
- *God, what do You say about this question?* (Am I significant, am I loved, what discomfort am I running from, are You trustworthy?)
- *God, please remind me of this truth, because my heart is weak and I'm feeling vulnerable right now.*
- *Lord, may Your words about this issue carry more weight and have more power than the words of the Enemy right now.*
- And finally, I will often find myself saying: *I choose NOT to give my heart to that right now; I recognize that it will not fill me; only Jesus can.*

Try this next time you are faced with temptation. I think it's a safe bet that by focusing on the heart, speaking directly to it, and inviting God into the process, you will be well on your way to bulldozing those hills.

A WORD ABOUT OUR PAIN, TRAUMA, AND INJURIES

I was recently talking with someone who is of Palestinian descent, who was sharing horrible stories of Israeli soldiers coming into his hometown and imprisoning kids simply because of their race.

This occurred after Israel felt threatened by Palestine and wanted to find a solution to the ongoing conflict between the two nations.

That occurred after Israel was granted permission to reestablish their country in the territory that was once considered Palestine; a result of a post-World War II decision.

That occurred after millions of Jewish people were executed in concentration camps around Nazi Germany.

Which occurred after Hitler decided that Jewish people were the main problem in Germany's economy.

Which happened after Germany was forced to pay incredible reparations as a result of a treaty signed in Versailles.

Which occurred after World War I and all of the bloodshed that happened during those horrific battles.

When we look at those things that we as humans are capable of, can we agree that we're all a bit messed up?

Adam and Eve eat some fruit, and sometime after, Cain kills Abel. Abraham sends Hagar and Ishmael off to die. Then he pawns his wife off to Pharoah. David sleeps with another man's wife and then sends her husband off to get killed in a dirty tactical move. Absalom rapes his sister; on and on the stories go. It's why some argue that the Bible must be true, because who in their right mind would put all of that ugly human behavior in a story that is trying to paint a picture of salvation and restoration? People do really awful things to each other. Sometimes it's tribe against tribe, but other times it's family against family; brother against brother or brother against sister. When these atrocities occur, we aren't honoring the fact that we, as humanity, are created in God's own image, and so we fight, war, rape, abuse, injure, slander, demolish, silence, domineer, and do all sorts of evil acts to and with one another. It's one of the reasons we all desperately need Jesus.

What if you were the victim of an evil act committed against you?

Often in these situations, trust and belief in Jesus might seem pretty hard to come by. You might feel alone, abandoned, or ignored. You might feel like God doesn't care and that He was absent when that atrocity happened to you. Or perhaps your injury wasn't as direct. Maybe your spouse walked out on you because of another lover. Or perhaps a close friend rejected you for reasons that are still a mystery.

The events of our lives impact how we see God.

My heart goes out to you, whatever your experiences have been. Our world is a broken place; one that is deeply fallen, and one where people commit terrible evils against each other. And while sometimes it might not seem like it, Jesus is still the answer.

It's why God sent angels to rescue Hagar and Ishmael while they were abandoned in the desert, even though He knew that Abraham's descendants (Ishmael and Isaac) would wage war against each other for thousands of years.[6]

---

[6] It is widely held that Isaac fathered the Jewish nation, while Ishmael fathered what is now Palestine.

If you are a victim of someone else's evil, please don't let that experience rob you of experiencing the true grace God wants to give you. And it's OK if you're mad at God for what happened. He can absolutely handle your questions, your tears, your "why's"; He can handle your anger, your doubts, and your fears. Consider all of these as an opportunity to connect with God.

I know that might seem abstract but remember that it's *people* who commit evil on other people; it is not God who does that.

So take your questions to Him (maybe your questions helped build the hill that needs to be bulldozed?), take your emotions to Him, and take your heart to Him. Because a God who was willing to sacrifice His own son in a brutal, torturous death knows what it's like to suffer evil at the hands of others. This God understands pain and abandonment. *(Consider Jesus' cry on the cross asking the Father why He had abandoned Him[7].)* Through it all, this God understands healing, because our God is a God of resurrection and of restoration.

And like Jesus emerging from the tomb, I believe God wants to do a restorative work in you as well.

If He can bulldoze the ultimate hill of death, there is no limit to what God is willing and able to bulldoze to reach you. It starts with approaching Him, bringing your questions to Him, and is made complete as we learn to trust Him and surrender our hearts to Him.

It takes work, it takes endurance, and it takes intentional persistence, but only through the cleared path can our hearts truly come alive.

---

[7] See Matthew 27:46.

A NOTE ABOUT THE BULLDOZED HILLS

When you look at a highway that's been freshly paved and see those areas that have been filled in to raise the road and also notice the areas that have been dug out to keep the road on its path, it's important to note that these provide evidence of the hill that used to be there. If the goal is a clear path of connection with God (i.e. a smooth highway), then that goal has been met.

Moreover, those *hills that used to be* that we see alongside the road should be viewed as monuments of God's work in your life as you and He worked together to rid yourself of your hills. Those hills have made an impact in your story, and no matter how hard you try, you really can't escape them. So let's stop trying to deny their existence and instead own them and own the progress and growth that God has helped you to realize.

Instead of pretending that they're not there, let's instead use those *hills that once were* to be a place where we can share our stories with freedom and to let those stories serve as inspiration to others who are struggling with those same hills.

It's why we talked about the voids first—being in community with others carries two great benefits: it helps us to be motivated to do the work on the hills, and also provides us a place to share for the benefit of others. In doing that, we not only help them along their path, but we also allow "God's bright glory to shine" (Isaiah 40:5).

And that, my friends, is the power of God working in and through our circumstances to help build His kingdom.

Now that I have that off my chest, let's take a look at the next step in the process: filling the ruts.

CHAPTER 5
FILLING THE RUTS

"After passing this morning through the valley in which we encamped last evening, the road brought us to the top of a high ridge, giving us a beautiful view of the mountains, running east and west, and parallel to the ridge over which we were passing. The sight was very fine, as these mountains were the first we had seen covered with pine since leaving Soda springs. This range is high and rugged, with its base well wooded; those to the left were equally as much so, while the Blue mountains to the northwest reared their peaks in dark blue masses high above the rest, and are covered with a growth of as beautiful timber as can be found between here and the Pacific ocean.."
—Osborne Cross, September 6, 1849

"We have good roads comparatively. We mean good roads if the sloughs are not belly deep and the hills not right straight up and down and not rock enough to turn the wagon over."
—Henry Allyn, August 11, 1853

Imagine what it would have been like to travel west during the covered wagon days.

I know, there are a few remnants of you out there who played the original Oregon Trail computer game, and you're already seeing the green-on-green screen, thinking about selling furs and buying food, but then Bam! You suddenly die of dysentery. Or is that just me whose mind goes there when I think of westward expansion?

What's interesting about travel during that period is that the weight of the wagon, coupled with its narrow wheels, would carve out small ruts in the path as they would make their way down the trail. As many travelers would journey along the same path, those ruts would gradually deepen. Add more and more travelers, and in some places you would have small trenches with barely enough height for the axles to pass beneath.

Did you know that our brains operate in a manner not unlike those old traveled roads?

When we practice a certain behavior, pattern, or habit, our brains create neural pathways not unlike ruts from a covered wagon. When we practice those behaviors, patterns, and habits more and more, those pathways get more and more ingrained in our brains. It's one of the reasons that long-standing habits are so difficult to break; our brains literally have pathways carved out in them that take considerable effort to re-pave, if you will.

So while some habits, like our morning cup of coffee, carry both neural pathways as well as addictive chemical responses in our brains, others, like watching the morning news while you drink that cup of coffee, have strictly neural impacts on our brains (without the accompanying chemical reactions).

With that in mind (yes, I really did pun that intentionally), let's take a look at the habits that we all form throughout our days.

Most of those habits are generally harmless, like that morning cup of coffee, or (mostly) even the news.

FILLING THE RUTS

Some are more insidious, like requiring some kind of sexual experience every night before you fall asleep, or needing alcohol to function at a social gathering. Now mind you, I have no problem with sex before sleep, or a drink at a social gathering; I'm talking about the difference between *enjoying* something and *requiring* something. The latter is evidence that you have a nice, deep neural pathway carved into your brain. And the secret to re-paving that is in replacing it with something else so you can carve a new pathway and provide space for the overgrowth to eventually cover over the old one.

So how do we address these ruts, these habits?

The first step is simply to pay attention. What do you find yourself habitually moving toward? These don't need to be destructive habits, just simply any practice or behavioral pattern that you find yourself repeating again and again. Some of these will tend to shift over time; for example, beginning in 2020, I began making the habit of checking various sources of news every morning after I had done my Bible and prayer time. (Sounds really holy, doesn't it?) But then I started noticing that I was spending more time in the news than I was in scripture and prayer. That act of noticing is the first step in filling the ruts.

I'd like to tell you that I had an instant shift in my approach to the news after this awareness. But let's be honest, I'm human just like the rest of us, and so my "noticing period" lasted several months.

It would look something like this: *wow, I noticed I spent more time in the news this morning than in scripture (again). I really should do something about that.* Rinse, wash, and repeat that line for several months, and that's pretty much what it looked like. Lots of noticing and zero change. So after I decided to get really determined, I started weaning myself from all of that extra time in the news each morning.

Success, right?

Well, sort of. After weaning myself from the morning news, I then started checking the news *during lunchtime* while I was eating. Turns out I ended up spending more time reading the lunchtime news than I had done previously during the morning routine. Ugh.

And those of you who are into the psychology of our *whole being* will notice that it might not be the healthiest habit to associate food with news, especially when so much of what's out there is absolutely terrible.

Continuing on with this practice could result in linking *food* with *terrible news.*

Now there's a great formula for overall emotional health and well-being, right?

EXAMINING OUR HABITS

Let's start by simply examining our habits and writing them down in our journal (hope you bought a big one). Be as granular as you need to be.

Mine might look something like this:

> *Wake up, turn off alarm clock, stumble downstairs.*
>
> *Start hot water kettle, weigh out coffee beans.*[1]

---

[1] I may have lost some of you who prefer a big-box coffee brewer, or even worse—instant coffee—but trust me, my morning pour-over coffee routine has become such a part of me that I even take my coffee equipment with me on vacation. I know. Pray for me. I need professional help.

FILLING THE RUTS

Make pour over, taking time to smell the bloom of the coffee.[2]

Take coffee to couch, open Bible.

Stare off into space while I sip coffee for 3-4 minutes; allow brain and eyes to wake up.

Read a passage in the Bible, meditate on it, pray through it.

Close Bible, pray about my day, my family, my work, and others.

Grab phone, check the following (in this order):

- *Text messages*
- *Bank account balance*
- *Emails*
- *Social media (3-5 min max)*
- *ESPN app (3-5 min max)*

Go potty.

Get gym clothes on.

Go to the gym.

Get home, shower up, start the next lengthy set of habits.

Each of these in the list above is a part of what I call my "morning routine", but essentially they are all habits. If you don't believe me,

---

[2] Yes, I really do this every morning. That aroma has a way of welcoming the day and reminding me of how grateful I am that God gave us the pleasures of taste and smell. Honestly!

try hanging out with me when any one of these steps gets disrupted; it can tend to affect my entire day. *(I know–pray for my family, and my wife in particular, as she apparently is married to a very fragile person.)*

So, as you start listing your habits, you might not be quite as granular as I was above, but you might highlight the big items:

Coffee

Bible

Prayer

Phone

Exercise

The goal is simply to get them down on paper so you can start to analyze them, and in particular, their merit (or value) in your life.

EXAMINING THEIR VALUE

Once you have your habits listed down, it's time to assess their "value add" (or "value detraction") to your life. A good metric is to measure these against their fruitfulness in helping create a clear path for God to do His best work in us.

One of my habits is regular exercise. Given my current time constraints, the best place for me to get that exercise is at the gym. Now, while that might not directly impact my communion with God (if anything, one could argue that the loud music, barrage of televisions, and fit people everywhere you look could be a spiritually healthy albeit a morally unhealthy habit). However, when I don't exercise, I notice that I am way less Christ-like during the rest of my day.

Without exercise, I am much more likely to let the stress of the day affect the way I treat those close to me. (I am not modeling Jesus' love for others well.) When I miss a workout, I am much more prone to worry and anxiety. (I am not allowing God to run the universe and instead I try to take over.) I am less joyful (and therefore not doing a particularly great job at reflecting God's glory and joy to those around me).

So while going to the gym doesn't provide the quiet places for my heart to ponder God's mysteries, it does provide all of the above benefits. As long as I also create intentional space for silence in my life, I have found that to be the much more beneficial routine. At the end of the day, I commune more intimately with God as a result of my regular exercise than if I were to skip it and replace it with extra piety.

A similar argument could be made for coffee. My morning cup provides a ritual of sorts that carves out space for me to engage the senses and engage God through those senses as I sip, read, pray, and repeat. I literally wake up to God every morning, and what is more intimate than that?

As you evaluate your habits, your conclusions might be different than mine. Maybe by working out in the morning, you're too tired to be an effective employee or a joyful spouse; maybe coffee spikes your anxiety and makes you a nervous wreck throughout the day.

Again, the measuring stick is this: Which habits bring *you* into a clearer path toward communion with God?

As long as none of our habits go against what God says is best (through scripture), you and I can differ all day long and both be right.

So, go through your list and mark a plus (+) next to each one that adds value to your life and clears the path to God. Put a minus (-) next to those which detract value and add clutter to your life. You might have a lot of minuses on your paper, and that's OK.

The next step is to prioritize these (both the good and the bad), making the good habits nonnegotiable (especially regular scripture reading and prayer).

As you prioritize your habits that clutter or detract from your experience of God, ask yourself which ones create the biggest ruts in your life? These would be recognized by the patterns that are the hardest to break and that seem to have the strongest hold on you. Let's start by dealing with those, and then work our way to the smaller ones.

Some very common ruts might be:

- Not getting enough sleep.
- Unhealthy diet or lifestyle (you and I both know no mortal being can pass up those sugar cookies at the market without snagging a container. Or two...)
- Lack of exercise (we all gotta move our bodies; God gave them to us to take care of, so if the gym is an issue, let's not throw the baby out with the bath water—find a way to work regular physical movement into your routine).
- Binge-watching Netflix, Hulu, Paramount +, or whichever other myriad streaming services are currently on your device.

Because we are integrated beings, our physical well-being affects our emotional and our spiritual well-being. We need to take all of these into account to make a clear path for God.

ELIMINATE THE MINUSES

I know some of you have habit superpowers, where you can simply make a decision on a Tuesday to either start a new habit or end an old one, and then you never miss a day for the next six years. The rest of us need to take baby steps sometimes. Deciding to quit something and then sticking with it is really, really difficult. Deciding to start something and sticking to it is also really, really difficult.

If you're wanting to add a new practice or routine, habit gurus will tell you to just start with two to three minutes each day. And while you habit superpower people might scoff at that, imagine what a few minutes of scripture reading could do for someone's life who hasn't picked up their Bible in years. Imagine what a few minutes of pushups might do for a person who hasn't exercised since their high school P.E. class. Imagine what two to three minutes of silence would do for all of our souls today. The point is, start small. Then start adding on to that, bit by bit.

A cycling magazine once had an article encouraging its readers to get out and ride–for ten minutes only–and after that they would have permission to get off the bike and quit their ride. I don't think anyone stopped after ten minutes. The joy of being on a bike, of feeling the wind against their face, the endorphin rush from the exercise–everyone kept riding longer than the minimum recommendation because they started to experience the benefit and joy of being on the bike.

If you struggle starting new habits, start small and build up from there.

Now, some of you might be wondering why I would start a section called "eliminate the minuses" by talking about *starting* things. It's because bad habits are so stinking hard to break, but way less difficult if we replace those habits with something new and good. It's why smokers who are trying to quit often turn to chewing gum as a way to stay busy while avoiding cigarettes.

It's not enough to not think about something or to stop doing something; we need to *replace* that spot in our mind, or that habit and pattern, with something else.

Now that we've identified the ruts in our lives, we may have been able to quit some and might be struggling with others. It's OK; this is normal. The reason many of us form less-than-healthy habits in the first place is that they are, on some level, desirable and oftentimes addicting. So, like the chewing gum, let's figure out some ways to replace the unhealthy habit with a healthy one. Let's begin by tapping into some healthy spiritual habits that can make a world of difference in our lives and in our hearts. It's how we fill the ruts and clear the path.

Let's look at some tried and true practices (called "Spiritual Disciplines") that saints throughout the ages have made a habit out of to better connect with God.

SOME SPIRITUAL PRACTICES TO TRY

Remember the analogy of the doctor telling you that you need to lose weight? You're either going to decide to eat healthier and get more exercise, or you're going to decide not to. Ultimately, the outcome rests solely in your hands and is also affected by how much you believe what the doctor is saying; if you think they're full of nonsense, you go on about your regular routines. If, on the other hand, you think that what they are advising has merit, you consider changing your current habits in exchange for healthier ones.

The habit of eating unhealthy foods and neglecting exercise forms a version of you that is overweight. The habit of a healthy diet and regular exercise forms a version of you that loses pounds.

We are all being formed.

We are all being formed by our environment, our friendships, our coworkers, by social media, the news, TV shows, and by music.

Don't believe me?

Try listening to country music for an afternoon and tell me you don't suddenly start thinking about whiskey more. Give Hip Hop a try and tell me you don't start viewing the world through a different lens than you had going in. Maybe it even makes you angry as you listen. Spend an afternoon listening to worship music and notice what happens on the inside.

I've never smoked a cigarette in my life.

But there was one time, during a summer while I was in college, that I actually stopped by the gas station on my way home from work—not to fill up my tank, but to buy a pack. Why? What would prompt someone to willingly stop to pick up a pack of cigarettes when I had never tried one before in my life? The answer? My work environment. I had been working at a job where literally everyone else smoked. I think it was a way to both pass the time and manage stress (or boredom).

My first week on the job was disgusting. I have always been repulsed by cigarette smoke (I was around it a *ton* when I was a kid; multiple grandparents smoked like chimneys) so that first week brought back all of those familiar smells that I never found attractive. But fast forward several weeks, and after hanging out with these guys for several hours each day, several days each month, I started finding that the smell started having a pull on me.

Maybe it really does help with boredom?

Maybe it really does ease the stress?

Maybe it is a way to fit in better with these guys?

And so I stopped at that gas station. (It was a Texaco, near The Boulevard and 4th street in Yucaipa, CA for the doubters out there.) I honestly can't remember if I got out of the car or not, but I do remember that I never actually went into the store.

Why?

In a moment of clarity, I found myself asking the question: *Do you want to be a smoker? Is this the type of person you want to become?*

Now, a quick side note: I have some very good, longtime friends who still smoke. It has not affected our friendship at all, so please do not misplace my question above with judgment against smokers. If you're a smoker, we all love you. We all have habits that aren't super healthy, so no judgment here. It was simply a question from me, to me, about what type of habits I wanted to employ for that season of my life. And so because of that question, I decided to keep my wallet in my pocket and drive away. My motivation was that *this is not the type of person I want to be*. So while being around my coworkers *formed* a desire to smoke cigarettes, something larger took over and prevented me from giving it a go.

You might not be surrounded by smokers, but you may be surrounded with several other coworkers who have side relationships with people other than their spouses. Maybe they even brag about their romantic weekend getaways while their unsuspecting spouse stays home with the kids. I would imagine, over time, you might start to think that a side hustle like that wouldn't be such a terrible thing. You might even begin to justify that it would ultimately be healthy for your marriage, as you wouldn't be placing such a burden on your spouse to meet all of your needs.

Maybe you're around people who have no problem judging others who aren't like them, and you find yourself replacing curiosity with curses, heaping judgment on "them" before you ever actually get a chance to know them or hear their reasoning behind what they believe on a particular topic.

We are all being formed by outside influences.

The big question is, what are you doing to combat the formation that this world is putting on you?

Or are you content simply outsourcing your formation to those friends, coworkers, Hollywood executives, music producers, and so on?

I hope and pray that you find the motivation to take your own formation seriously, and that you find joy in the process of partnering with God to form the type of person He has in mind for you when He looks adoringly at you.

REGULAR BIBLE READING

Since we are all being formed by something, why not carve out space for part of our "input" to be directly from God Himself?

The best way to do that is through the reading of scripture.

When you think about how much has changed in the past few thousand years, it's remarkable to note that scripture hasn't.

Scripture is timeless, because God is timeless, and God has given us scripture to lend some insight on a few really critical topics:

- How He relates to humanity.
- How we relate to Him.
- How we're all a bit of a broken mess.
- How His plan has been for human flourishing since the very beginning.

There are countless others, of course, but the bottom line is this: when I read the Bible, I notice that I learn about God's heart toward His people, I learn about my heart and its propensity to wander, and I learn about how God's plan is always a plan of redemption and restoration.

It is truly a plan of Good News.

And since we have this amazing tool at our disposal that generations of Christ-followers did not have access to (think about it: the printing press wasn't invented until just over 600 years ago—invented to make copies of the Bible, by the way), why wouldn't we capitalize on the opportunity to read it for ourselves? But sadly, more Bibles collect dust on bookshelves, sit in hotel room drawers, and get ignored in app-based notifications than we can count.

Imagine what just ten minutes each morning of God-based input could do for your day.

It's why Bible reading is one of those habits that I commit to regardless of whether I'm traveling, working, healthy, sick, whatever—as David said, like the deer pants for water, so my soul pants for God[3]. All of our souls do; the act of recognizing this truth has real potential to transform our lives.

If you struggle with reading your Bible, I would encourage you to simply try it for a week. Set your alarm to wake up ten minutes earlier than usual; you won't notice the sleep difference, but I have a strong hunch you'll notice a change in other ways. See how your outlook changes as you are providing intentional space to be formed by God before the world gets its shot at you.

SILENCE

We talked about this briefly, but the practice of silence is really based on shutting out all of the noise in our lives in order to create space for God to reveal anything He wants to show us. It is a conscious decision to block out the input (music, television, news, notifications on our phones) and instead create a clear path for God to speak. Consider that silence is allowing your mind to take a little vacation.

Have you ever come back from a restful getaway with renewed energy, creative ideas, and new solutions to problems that seemed to come from out of nowhere? It's because your brain had some time to unplug from all of the stimuli, which provided space for it to operate in the creative realm. Turning off the noise allows for creativity to happen. It's like putting your brain in Do Not Disturb mode so you aren't interrupted by all of the many things that vie for your attention.

---

[3] Psalm 42:1.

When we practice silence, we can do this in small chunks throughout the day, whether it's waiting in line at the store, pausing to just catch our breath for a minute before heading into that next meeting, or taking an evening away from your phone and TV so you can remember what it's like to be human again.

Silence also creates space for God to bring things to the surface that He has been wanting to make us aware of. These could be areas where you need His healing help, or they could be things He wants to celebrate with you.

Imagine being so busy and distracted that you miss out on a "well done" that He wants to say to you? Imagine being so busy and distracted that you miss out on an opportunity to become more healed and whole?

As Dallas Willard once said, *we must ruthlessly work to eliminate hurry from our lives*, and taking moments of silence is a direct affront to our propensity to be busy, distracted, and rushed. Silence helps create a clear path for God to do some of His best work.

LISTENING PRAYER

Some of you may come from traditions where you were told that God gave us His word in the Bible, and He doesn't speak to His people in any ways other than that anymore. While I can appreciate that the aim of that statement is to prevent people from speaking for God (please be very careful if someone claims this), claiming that God doesn't still speak simply isn't consistent with what Scripture tells us:

> The one who enters by the gate is the shepherd of the sheep. The gatekeeper opens the gate for him, and the sheep listen to his voice. He calls his own

sheep by name and leads them out. When he has brought out all his own, he goes on ahead of them, and his sheep follow him because they know his voice.

—John 10:2–4 (NIV)

Now, a critical caveat: Implied in the text is that the sheep know the shepherd's voice. And how can you know the shepherd's voice? You have to spend time listening to it. And the best way to listen to the shepherd's voice is to spend time in scripture (it's why we start with that practice first).

Too many people have spoken a word, saying it was from God, that stood in direct opposition to scripture. If someone *ever* tells you that God told them something that happens to contradict Scripture, it's the person, not God, who is the liar. That person was deceived, and you need to distance yourself from them so you don't lose your bearing.

I cannot stress this enough.

I have been in small groups with our church when someone said something like, "Yeah, I prayed about it, and God said [this sinful behavior] was OK. So since He told me that, I'm going to go with that." That poor, sweet person was deceived. God will never contradict Himself[4]. He cannot, because Truth cannot contradict truth; the second it does, it is no longer truth.

So how do we know if something we think we hear from God is really God? We test it against scripture. And how do we know our scripture? We read it.

---

[4] See 2 Timothy 2:13.

I've literally had people quote me verses in the Bible that don't even exist. One of the more famous is *God helps those who help themselves.* That verse is not in the Bible, and because it is not in scripture, I hold it as a saying, but I do not hold it as truth.

OK, now that I'm all worked up about people misrepresenting God, let's talk about how we can create space for Him to represent Himself to us.

When we practice Listening Prayer, we practice a posture of humility, of quietude, and of patient waiting.

Listening Prayer provides a space for us to hear from God rather than for us to be the one doing all the talking as we make request after request to Him. It takes the focus away from one-way communication and instead creates space for a much deeper, more intimate two-way conversation. Imagine how much fun being in a one-sided relationship would be? The aim of this practice is to create space for our relationship with God to become two-sided, where He speaks to us because He loves us and wants us to become all that He has designed us to be.

So how do we do it?

We start by removing all distractions. That usually means we go to a still, quiet place where we can be away from our phones, away from noise, and away from other people. It doesn't have to be a retreat center or a national park, it can simply be a room in your house or even a closet—just somewhere where you can block out the noise and focus on God.

For me, we recently moved into a house with a way-too-large closet in our bedroom. Since my wardrobe consists mainly of shorts and t-shirts, I have an inordinate amount of space on my side of the

FILLING THE RUTS

closet. So I have taken to using that space for quiet prayer. In fact, I recently told my wife that if she came around the corner and saw me motionless, crouching on the floor and face down, to please refrain from calling 911–at least until I was done praying.

I usually start my time with a prayer of surrender:

> *Jesus, I give everyone and everything to You. I give You all my burdens, all of my worries, any distractions, and all of the good and bad things that would distract me from you right now.*
>
> *I confess any sin in my life now* (be specific) *and I lay these at Your feet, Jesus.*
>
> *I surrender every outcome, every decision, every event in my future to You, and I ask that You would be Lord over my life right now and always.*
>
> *I surrender my will and my desires, and I pray that You would help align them with Yours, Jesus.*
>
> *Please speak to me here, and may I be open to what You have to say.*[5]

I then wait, removing any pressure to hear anything in that exact moment, and instead focus on who God is, who He says I am (and who I am not). Oftentimes, He will reveal things to me in that space.

---

[5] This is an adaptation of a prayer from John Eldredge and Wild at Heart ministries. If you don't know who they are, you are missing out, big-time. Consider downloading the One Minute Pause app for starters and watch how it transforms your life.

It might simply be that He loves me. Or sometimes He says He is proud of me. Other times He confronts me with something I said or did, or a thought I had that needs dealing with. When that happens, I confess those things to Him, and then I reset by asking if there is anything else. Anything else He wants to say to me, reveal to me, or any specific action or direction I need to take in my life.

True story, this very book you're holding is a result of a time of Listening Prayer and my efforts at trying to be faithful to share a message He had laid on my heart after a personal season of significant decluttering.

End your time of prayer with gratitude, and use that experience to fuel your soul.

FASTING

Contrary to what I observe on most of the roads and highways in Southern California, "fasting" is not seeing if you can out-maneuver the other cars on the road, legally or otherwise, to get a few feet ahead of the next driver.

Fasting is the act of denying yourself something that you typically rely on, in order to replace those desires with a movement toward God. It most often involves food (my recommendation), but doesn't have to. When we fast (let's use food as an example), we purposely choose not to eat food for a period of time (typically a day) in order to focus more on God. Whenever I have really big decisions to make, I will often find myself setting aside time to pray and fast over those decisions before I make the final call. It's a way of telling my body that my appetite is not my god, and it's a way of telling my soul that God is more than enough to fill me completely. That very act of controlling your appetite, what I call exercising your "no muscle", is something incredibly powerful.

Imagine you are walking through the grocery store, and you see those heaven-sent sugar cookies up front. Of course you are going to want them, but when you walk past them and say "no" to them, you have demonstrated a measure of self-control that will have ripple effects on other areas of your life. You greatly desire the cookies—you say no, exercising that muscle—and then when the next larger temptation comes your way, you have confidence in your ability to resist. And so you do. That act of saying no gives you more strength for the next temptation, and so on.

If you're skeptical, test my hypothesis and see if I'm wrong. (By the way, saying "no" to "saying no" is not a recommended form of exercising your "no muscle".)

When we fast, we exercise that "no muscle" and, like other aspects of this chapter, we replace the desire for food with something else.

When fasting, I notice that I will often crave all kinds of random foods throughout my day. If you didn't know better you might think I was pregnant. But each time I crave food, I will simply pray: *Lord, I am hungry right now. May my hunger for You be just as intense as my hunger for this meal. Fill me with Your divine presence, Lord, and may I be satisfied by that.* By denying myself food and focusing that desire into a prayerful approach to God, I am both exercising self-control over my body (my appetites) and giving God a primary place in my day.

During mealtimes, I will spend that time praying, offering those big decisions up to God. It's often a prayer of surrender, asking God to make His will known, and that I would be faithful and courageous enough to follow it.

And when I break the fast (usually the next day) with a meal, I notice all kinds of gratitude for the simple things, even if it's eggs and toast, and I give God thanks for providing me with His sustenance (spiritually) and for providing food (practically).

It's truly a beautiful thing.

And it's not necessarily popular, because we live in a society that denies itself *nothing*. Think about it: Whatever you want, you can basically have it right now. Want to travel? Go on Insta and YouTube and look up new and exciting travel destinations, where literally everything is perfect and you don't have to go anywhere to "experience" it. Want to buy that latest book you've been wanting to read? Pull up Amazon, buy a digital download, and start reading it right now (and you don't have to fight for a parking space at the bookstore!) Want a sexual experience? Hop on that phone and search for whatever it is you're desiring at the moment.

Too real?

Can we see how exercising the no muscle would be a good thing here? Learning to say no is not only a lost art, but it's a real spiritual discipline. Remember, Jesus said:

> "If any of you wants to be my follower, you must give up your own way, take up your cross, and follow me."
>
> —Matthew 16:24 (NLT)

This act of *giving up our own way* is exactly the same thing as exercising our no muscle. And like any other kind of exercise, it takes some work, some practice, and lots of dedication in order to do it well. But isn't the payoff worth it? When we exercise our no muscle—when we fast—we not only gain control over our appetites, but we also open ourselves up to hear more clearly from God.

It's that whole Listening Prayer thing on steroids.

When I fast, I *expect* to hear from God. I am intentionally seeking Him throughout my day. I am constantly turning my appetites over to Him, asking Him to be Lord over them. And when I fast, I often notice interesting and unique ways in which God meets me with my questions. Sometimes it's through another person, sometimes it's an unexpected email; oftentimes God reveals certain people I need to talk to in order to gain wisdom in making my big decision. Every time, no matter the outcome, I feel closer to God. Whether or not He has revealed His answer in that moment, I still notice that I feel closer to Him at the end of that day.

Why?

Because I approached Him constantly throughout the day. Because I admitted that I am needy and that my soul needs Him more than it needs its independence. Because I submitted my very body to a practice, modeled by Jesus Himself, that draws us closer in union with the Father.

Now, while fasting from food is the most common (and my personal favorite), I have known people to participate in all kinds of other fasts[6]:

- Fasting from social media.
- Fasting from TV shows (or from television altogether).
- Fasting from the news.

All of these are valid fasts, as far as I'm concerned. But the real test is not whether I think it's valid, but whether it draws you closer to God.

---

[6] If we're being technical here, these "other fasts" would be in the category of "abstinence" rather than fasting, but for simplicity I've lumped them into the same discussion.

When you fast from social media, perhaps this practice brings to light that you have placed too much significance and self-worth in what others think about you; God brings that to the surface during your time away from your social accounts, and allows you the opportunity to bring that sense of significance to Him so He can speak into it.

When you fast from TV shows, you might begin to notice that all sitcoms are written specifically so that the viewer does not have closure at the end (so you'll be drawn to watching the next episode), and you notice that the lack of closure feels too much like other aspects of life, and so maybe you notice that you are more relaxed without them. You find that God can provide more answers and peace and fulfillment than those TV shows, and in doing so, your soul is refreshed.

Perhaps as you fast from the news you notice that all news outlets are really only out for one thing: advertising dollars. And the only way to ensure they get advertising dollars is to ensure that their content is constantly playing with your emotions—toggling you between anger, fear, anxiety, and concern. Taking a break from that allows the steadfastness of God to enter in and take the place that the media-created anxiety had, and you suddenly feel more security in your soul.

Whatever you choose to fast from, do it for a predetermined period of time (I recommend up to 24 hours for food, and up to a week or more for the media-related fasts), and each time your desires turn to that thing, bring them instead to God. Allow Him to minister to you in that place, and open yourself up to whatever He would have for you as you practice denying yourself and following the path of Jesus.

Oh, and if you choose to fast from coffee, for the love of all that is holy, please let your family, friends, and coworkers know. While scripture says to keep your fasting private between you and God only[7], I think there is grace for this particular category. Because when someone is suddenly taken off caffeine, most of the world feels that ripple effect in the person's mood, their ability to roll with the punches, and their all-around well-being.

I'm joking. Sort of.

Make sure when you fast that you are doing so in a manner that brings you closer to God, and in a manner that is also considerate of others. Maybe your daughter's 16th birthday isn't the best day to fast from sweets, right? Let's keep in mind that it's her day also.

WORSHIP

Worship is a heart thing.

We all worship. If you don't believe me, go to a playoff game of any professional sport and watch the fans chant the superstar's name in unison. Take a look at the biggest social media influencers and tell me that people don't worship whatever they post about. Or, to bring it closer to home, go through your bank statement, noticing the patterns of what you spend your money on, and something tells me it'll point to those things that you worship.

Since worship is a heart thing, the practice of spiritual worship often involves music and singing, but it also involves the posture of our hearts as we do so. When you sing worship songs at church or listen to worship music on your way to work, what happens in your heart? Does it move you to weep at times? To celebrate God's goodness? To

---

[7] See Matthew 6:16–18.

be moved at the notion of His utter majesty? Or is it simply a series of notes and words strung together to fill the time before the sermon?

By the way, attending church in person is a really great way to engage in worship. It doesn't force the issue, but it does provide the clearest path to ushering in that experience. Nothing is more powerful in worship than a congregation singing from the heart, together; if you haven't been to church in a long time, you're truly missing out.

So what happens in genuine worship?

- Worship reminds us of who God is.
- Worship reminds us that we belong to God, not to ourselves.
- Worshiping with other believers reminds us that we are not alone.
- Worship reminds us that God can be trusted with our souls.

Now, worship doesn't just have to be limited to music; I have had incredible worship experiences while out in nature, gazing at the stars or at mountain meadows or at majestic waterfalls. My only word of caution is, when in nature, make sure you are worshiping the Creator rather than the creation. I speak from personal experience here. Worshiping creation will disappoint; if the waterfall isn't flowing as strongly as it was last year, you will find yourself disappointed. But if you are worshiping the Creator, you will notice all kinds of other things about that waterfall than its variable flow rate. You will notice how God has created beauty for beauty's sake; you will notice how the water sustains life below the falls, and how God has sustained that over the various seasons that the water has flown full or light. You will notice that the God who created all of this keeps all of life in motion, and what a beautiful thing that is.

Worship is a heart thing, and we can have influence over our hearts in the things that capture our focus, our attention, and our adoration.

SOLITUDE AND RETREAT

While this list is nowhere near exhaustive, we will end on the idea of solitude and retreat.

There are times where it is actually really good to get away, by yourself, for alone time with God. These times are what the saints have called Solitude and Retreat. It's like the culmination of all of the above, tied up with a nice, neat bow: you get time for intentional Bible reading, you get silence, you get Listening Prayer, you can choose to fast, you often find yourself worshiping. It's really great.

Although "retreat" may sound fancy and potentially expensive, all it takes is for you to carve out a predetermined span of time to focus on all of these things.

And it doesn't have to cost you a lot of money.

Personally, I usually just pack my backpack with a Bible, a journal, a few snacks (unless I'm fasting), and water. After packing, I throw on my hiking shoes, drive to the local mountains, and find a trail where I'm the least likely to run into other humans for a while. I hike, I pray, I stop when I feel God is asking me to stop. I notice nature, I thank God for nature, I read scripture, I pray some more, and so on. Sometimes my retreat time is more active; other times it is more still. It really depends on what God invites me into during that time. I really recommend that you try it. It's kind of like choosing to spend the day with a good friend and you have moments of conversation together, moments of silence, moments of joy, and perhaps moments of sorrow. The point is that you are sharing that focused time *together*, focused on the relationship.

Retreat with God is just that: focused time with Him, while allowing Him to dictate the agenda and not you.

Some common rhythms of retreat are:

- A half-day each month. Spend the morning with God, somewhere local, and then re-engage with your friends and family later that afternoon.
- A full day each quarter. Extend your half-day and see how God meets you in that extended time.
- An overnighter each year. Extend one of your retreat times to include an overnighter (if you're married, make sure your spouse is on board with this first). Be intentional about planning that one so that you aren't overnighting in a place that will throw you into temptation, but rather a place that will foster a greater dependence on, and communion with, God.

The point with all of these is to look forward to spending intentional time with God. It's totally appropriate to bring questions, to bring thoughts and ideas, but it's equally important to hold your plans with an open hand, being willing to shift your agenda if God has something else in mind for that time.

It's all about simply clearing the path and enjoying the fellowship with the Creator. Nothing else.

CHAPTER 6

WORK TIRELESSLY TO REMOVE THE ROCKS

Thunder in the desert!
"Prepare for God's arrival!
Make the road straight and smooth,
a highway fit for our God.
Fill in the valleys,
level off the hills,
Smooth out the ruts,
clear out the rocks.
Then God's bright glory will shine
and everyone will see it.
Yes. Just as God has said."

—Isaiah 40:1–5 (MSG)

The other day as I was driving by the high school track I noticed something peculiar in the construction area. It was something that looked like a large metal lean-to but with a meshed roof. Next to it was a very large pile of rocks. Not boulders, but rocks. I'd like to think they were small enough for someone like me to pick up without the use of any special equipment, but maybe that's just the "post gym workout" version of me talking. In reality, they are probably small but mighty, requiring mechanical scoops to actually move them around.

But the lean-to continued to baffle me, until I finally realized that it was a giant sifter used for the dirt that was later to be used as the foundational base of the track and field.

What seems to be happening is that the tractors are scooping up the entire track and its field, section by section, and throwing it through the sifter in order to comb out all of the impurities in the dirt. What results is a pile of rocks on one side, and a pile of really nice dirt on the other. The rocks get discarded, and the really nice dirt (and only the really nice dirt) gets used for the project, allowing for a really smooth base over which the track and accompanying field will eventually be laid.

Again, we're so glad I'm not in charge of this project because I would never think to go through the dirt with that much scrutiny. I would be inclined to scrape away whatever rocks I might see on the surface, but apparently that's not enough for a quality project; the removal of the rocks needs to go deep in order to ensure the proper foundation for the completed field.

Isaiah was a tremendous prophet, and I'm guessing he would have been a better project manager for this track than I would have been.

After we've done the hard work to fill the valleys (voids) in our lives, remove the hills (sins), and fill the ruts (habits and practices), we now get to do the painstaking work of removing the rocks so that the path can be smooth enough to be paved.

You've identified the voids that you are filling with things other than God and have begun to practice filling them with more and more of what He offers (including church and Christian community).

WORK TIRELESSLY TO REMOVE THE ROCKS

This process has revealed sinful patterns in your life that you have begun working hard to identify and to remove, replacing them with less destructive behaviors.

You have begun paying attention to what's going on in your heart, making the conscious decision to not give your heart to those things that entangle[1], and instead to deliberately offer the pieces of your heart to Jesus so He can redeem and restore these places.

This awareness has also led you to examine your habits and whether they position yourself to engage with Jesus more intentionally, or whether they slowly nudge you off course in your journey to creating a clear path for intimacy with God.

You may be thinking: I've done all these things, I'm seeing some positive results, and now you're telling me there's *more work to be done*? Yeah, I am.

The reason I say this is because Scripture says there's more and God desires such incredible closeness with you that He is willing to point out every single thing that stands in the way of you experiencing Him in His fullness.

The very thing our hearts deeply long for is that they experience God. Consider all the ways we seek connection, adventure, intimacy, beauty, belonging, significance, identity—these are all rooted in our hearts' deep awareness that we are no longer walking with God in Eden. And so we create false Edens here, but they never live up to their promise because our false Edens are finite and simply cannot measure up to the Infinite. And because God desires the best for each of us, and that "best" is a restoring of the closeness that was felt in Eden, He is willing to show us everything that stands in the way of that level of intimacy with Him.

---

[1] See Hebrews 12:1–2.

Thank God for that.

Hopefully by now, as you've personally engaged with some of the practices in this book, you have noticed periods of closeness with God that have refreshed you, filled you, and encouraged you. Hopefully you have begun experiencing the love and joy of God the Father as He partners with you to clear the path to your heart.

I pray these experiences with God continue to encourage you to keep on clearing the path, because this next step, clearing the rocks, just might be the most difficult (and the most rewarding) stage of the process.

ASK GOD TO REVEAL THE ROCKS

I used to be a high school teacher, and no matter how well I taught a lesson, how thoroughly I prepared, and how excellently I delivered the content, none of that mattered unless the students did the work to actually learn it. As a teacher, my responsibility was to do my best to facilitate learning, but at the end of the day it was up to the students to take what I had taught, put it into practice, and learn by doing the work.

Occasionally I would get a student who would approach me and ask if I could review their work to see where they were getting a problem or concept wrong. I was able to look over their efforts, point out what needed to change, allow them the space and time to rework the problem, and then come back to me for another round of corrections. These students—the ones who would take the initiative to come to me for help—were the ones I imagined would have the brightest future, because they were *teachable*.

I have gone decades of my life without recognizing the

WORK TIRELESSLY TO REMOVE THE ROCKS

importance of this quality personally, because I somehow thought I was above all that, but as I've gotten older (and hopefully a bit wiser), it's this *teachable* trait that provides people the best advantage at reaching their full potential.

In a similar way, when we approach God to ask Him for help in identifying our rocks (or our ruts, hills, or valleys), we not only demonstrate that we are teachable, but we also get extra time with the Teacher. We are invited into a one-on-one relationship with the One who knows infinitely more than we do, who can envision infinitely more than we can for our lives, and who cares enough to guide us along that process.

If we ask.

Let's start there. Let's see it as an invitation for intimacy rather than a beat-down session where a harsh God is going to point out all of the areas where you have fallen short[2].

So let's define the rocks: these are those small, beneath-the-surface things that keep us from experiencing God in all of His fullness. They dot the path but might not be so noticeable at first.

You might have read enough Scripture to have solid doctrine, you might have great habits and practices, you may have worked hard to fill your voids with godly things, you may have worked hard to remove much of the sin in your life.

---

[2] This approach is not uncommon, and yet is often rooted in past experiences shaping our current view of God. In the next chapter we'll allow space for God to reveal who He is to us, setting aside who we think He is. My prayer is that this process will be incredibly healing for you.

But even with these things, I would venture that there is more that your heart can experience here[3].

And this *more* is where our hearts can come truly alive if we allow ourselves space and time to process these things with God, work on them together, and enjoy the intimacy that results in engaging with Emmanuel throughout the process.

One of the fallacies of Christianity is that we have to have everything 100% right in order to experience the Kingdom of God. That simply isn't consistent with scripture—the Bible makes it clear that Jesus has already made us right with God through his death and resurrection[4]. The process of growth is really an invitation to intimacy as God reveals more and more of Himself (and of us) as we intentionally walk with Him.

Let's break down some of the areas where we find rocks in our lives. Recall, these are the beneath-the-surface things that keep us from God and can therefore be difficult to locate. I am not claiming to provide an exhaustive list (remember, that's work that you and Jesus get to do together), but I will break them down into these two primary categories:

Rocks that originate from our *Fear*.

Rocks that originate from our confusion with *Identity*.

---

[3] I say that with confidence, because as we've already discussed, God is infinite and by definition, there is always *more* in the infinite.
[4] See Romans 3:22–26.

ROCKS THAT ORIGINATE FROM OUR FEAR

> *"Aslan is a lion- the Lion, the great Lion." "Ooh" said Susan. "I'd thought he was a man. Is he-quite safe? I shall feel rather nervous about meeting a lion" ... "Safe?" said Mr Beaver ... "Who said anything about safe? 'Course he isn't safe. But he's good. He's the King, I tell you."*
>
> — C.S. Lewis, *The Lion, the Witch and the Wardrobe*[5]

In his epic allegory, C.S. Lewis points to the human heart so expertly: At our core, we all want to know if God can be trusted. And in a brilliant stroke of the pen, Lewis shows two amazing things about God: *No, of course he isn't safe* but He is *good*.

Oh, if we could just believe that in our hearts, how different might our lives be.

But no, we have a hard time believing God is good, because we've seen when He isn't safe. And because we have a tendency to misinterpret the meaning of His actions, we can sometimes err on the side of subtly wondering if perhaps He isn't good. And when we don't think God is good, we then assume control over our lives.

It's one of the main reasons, in my opinion, why the First Commandment is all about us not having any other gods. If we could allow God to be God (and therefore be the One who is in control), we would trust Him implicitly; but in order for us to trust Him implicitly, we need to trust that He is good. And around and

---

[5] *The Lion, the Witch and the Wardrobe* by CS Lewis © copyright 1950 CS Lewis Pte Ltd.
Extract reprinted with permission.

around we go. I'll talk more about why I don't think God is safe in a minute, but let's focus on the *is God good?* question first.

Life tends to throw us all kinds of surprises, doesn't it? Some might be, *surprise!* your close friends have thrown you a birthday party that you were unaware of. After the initial shock wears off, you feel special and loved and celebrated and seen. But sometimes life throws us other surprises.

Surprise! your company is downsizing and you no longer have a job and a means to support your family. *Surprise!* a loved one just found out she has cancer and the outlook is not good. *Surprise!* you just learned that your son is gay. *Surprise!* your teenage daughter is pregnant. *Surprise!* you just learned that your spouse has been involved in a romantic relationship for years and has been lying to you all this time.

It seems that we get way more bad surprises in life than we do good ones, right?

And while some well-meaning Christians might tell you that all of these are a result of our fallen world (which they are), when a surprise like this hits you between the eyes, that's not exactly helpful counsel while the wound is wide open, is it[6]?

How many people, after a lifetime of these types of bad surprises, mutter something like *when I get to Heaven, I've got a lot of questions for God; He's going to have to give me some answers when I get there …*

---

[6] For guidance on what helpful counsel would look like, look into the Ministry of Presence. Simply being with someone who is grieving, even if it means silence, can be an incredible way we can be the comforting presence of Jesus in the midst of their grief.

WORK TIRELESSLY TO REMOVE THE ROCKS

I get it.

Life is painful. Life is hard. Life is unpredictable. Life isn't safe.

Because of our fallen world, and because our past experiences shape our view of God, it can be exceptionally difficult to trust in His goodness during times of intense pain and questioning.

Many books have been written on this very subject, so I won't make a feeble attempt to answer these questions that others have already written so extensively about, but I will offer this: A main point of this book is to examine what is going on at the heart level inside us. I would offer that these heart-level questions are the very ones to bring directly to God.

If you've read the Psalms, this is exactly what happens. When King David is being hunted down, he cries out at a heart level to God, asking Him where in the world He's been and why He's not protecting David[7]. And yet David survived the hunt, because if he didn't, we wouldn't have those Psalms.

When David is feeling abandoned by God, and writes about it in Psalm 22, he also ends with a beautiful sense of God's future provision. Why such hope at the end of this Psalm when David starts it out with such incredible despair? *(I would strongly recommend you set down this book for a few minutes and really meditate on this beautifully powerful Psalm—it can be like water to a thirsty soul.)* I would argue that the turning point in the Psalm is when David, in his despair, begins to remember the ways God has provided for His people in the past.

This, I believe, is the key to unlocking the places in our heart that doubt God's goodness. When we look back on the past it usually lets

---

[7] See Psalm 7, among several others.

us in on where God was, how He was with us all along, and where He used that bad surprise to strengthen us, reveal something about us, and reveal more of who He is[8].

Keep in mind that we often misplace bad surprises as though they were sent from God Himself, or at least something He should have prevented, rather than something that occurred out of humanity's brokenness and God's fierce dedication to allowing humans free will in our actions and decisions.

The result? Because life doesn't go according to our script, we assume that God isn't good, for if He were, then our lives wouldn't be so painful.

The problem with that perspective (other than being incredibly short-sighted) is that when we assume we know what's good and what's bad, we are essentially jumping right in line behind Adam, taking a bite of the fruit and placing ourselves over and above God as author of our life's story.

And that, my friends, is one more example of the finite trying to take the place of the Infinite. It will always fail us and always leave us disappointed.

So—what do we do with this question about whether God is good?

My hope is that, as you have experienced more of God through this process of clearing the path to your heart, any existing walls of

---

[8] I say "usually" here, because sometimes there are especially traumatic events that we need to process with a trusted Spiritual advisor (like a Christian counselor, pastor, or Spiritual Director). When we experience trauma, a very fair question is to ask Jesus where He was during that event. I have heard some really powerful stories of healing when a person has been guided through this exercise. Oftentimes, Jesus is right there in the room with them, weeping alongside them, sharing in the pain and the grief.

distrust begin to break down as you experience more and more of His goodness.

My hope is also that, as you have ongoing, deeper questions about God's goodness, you start by reflecting back on all of the ways He has been good to you in the past (James, the brother of Jesus, said that all good gifts come from the Father[9]) and secondly, that you bring your questions to God and allow Him space to answer in His timing and in His gentleness.

Again, consider these questions as an invitation into intimacy.

I trust that as you bring these before God, He will grant you an increasingly greater awareness of His innate goodness, and that as you begin to trust in that more and more, you will be rewarded with the immeasurable fullness of God.

With that as a foundational backdrop, let's look at how this plays out.

OUR TENDENCY TO TAKE CONTROL

Fear can motivate us to do some pretty incredible things. From the practice of stockpiling toilet paper and ammunition during a pandemic, to the domineering of our children, the fear of bad things and of unforeseen circumstances can thrust us into a frantic position of always trying to maintain control of our environments.

One of the reasons we try to assume control is because we don't think God is wholeheartedly good and has our best in mind, and we conclude that we are all alone. When we operate out of this space, we try to manufacture predictable outcomes in nearly every aspect

---

[9] See James 1:17.

of our lives. We try to eliminate (or at the very least, mitigate) the bad surprises and will go to incredible measures to accomplish this.

Skeptical? Did 2020 teach us anything about how fear and control are so closely intertwined?

If you notice you try to control everything in your life (hint: that's all of us), you will want to work on your fear, and the first step to working on fear is to work on *surrender*. A very practical example of this would be to let your waiter choose his or her favorite menu item and let them serve that dish without you having any input in the decision[10]. At the core level, putting your trust in the server is a small act of surrender. And while they might not give you the perfect dish, my guess is it won't kill you and it probably won't taste bad either.

Isn't that what our base-level fears are all about? That the life event won't be to our liking, and that it might very well lead to some level of extreme discomfort and possibly even death. So if we can learn to trust our server at a restaurant, maybe that will give us a small victory in our learning to trust in God. We would all intellectually admit that God is far more trustworthy than our server, and yet we have such a hard time offering Him complete surrender.

But here's the good news: As we practice filling our voids, bulldozing our hills, filling the ruts, and identifying our rocks, these very actions build trust in God because they foster a partnership with Him.

As we work on these bigger issues, we can begin to develop the trust to allow Him access to those smaller (and yet far deeper, equally important) little rocks that need to be sifted out in order for us to commune with God on that deeper level, and in doing so, live out

---

[10] I predict some of you might be literally twitching as you read this suggestion...

the life He intends for us—one of joy and fulfillment (which stand in direct opposition to our fears).

So, for these rocks of wrestling control from God, start by admitting your fears, writing them down and inviting God to speak directly into them.

It's okay to ask, *God, I fear that I will be left all alone in life; is that true? Am I alone?* In fact, I'd suggest that the way God will answer that honest and vulnerable prayer will be something far more beautiful than either of us could imagine at this moment. Because God is *good* and He desires goodness for you. If He didn't want Adam alone in the Garden, He certainly doesn't want you alone right now, and if you extend the tender invitation to speak into that, He will.

A simple prayer might look something like this:

> *Dear Jesus, I admit my tendency to try to take control over my life. I admit that You and You alone are God, and I am not. Minister to my heart in this place, Lord, and remind me that You are good and that I can trust You with every detail of my life.*
>
> *I surrender these details and these fears that cause me to wrestle control, and I ask that You would grow my faith as I learn a greater level of dependence on You, God.*
>
> *For I trust You, I trust Your heart to me. As the Centurion prayed, Lord I believe; help me with my unbelief.*
>
> *Thank you for being a Good Father; I surrender myself completely to You.*
>
> *In Jesus' name, amen.*

ROCKS THAT STEM FROM OUR MISUNDERSTANDING OF IDENTITY

When we live a life of trying to control every outcome, essentially denying God His sovereignty, we violate the First Commandment of keeping God in first position in our lives. When we operate out of that space and out of the fear-based choices that originate from our feeling alone in the world, all kinds of screwy things happen as it relates to our identity. We'll go more in depth on this in chapter 8, but for now can we agree that we all struggle with crafting false images of ourselves that we offer to others?

This stems from our fears of inadequacy *(I'm not enough)* and shame *(if people knew the real me they wouldn't love me)* and is another way we assume control over our lives.

We make terrible gods, don't we?

When left to our own devices, we end up crafting all of these images as a way to cover our shame. These fig leaves are often referred to as the False Self.

A good starting point is to ask God to reveal those images you have created for yourself that serve as a means of guarding your true self from the world[11]?

Some common False Selves might look like this:

- "I've got it all together" *(hides our sense of inadequacy).*
- "I'm just really awkward" *(lowers others' expectations of you and hides your real value).*

---

[11] More on this in chapter 8. This is NOT referring to us choosing our own identity, but rather, our "true self" originating from God Himself–who He says we are and who we could become; not what we say we are and want to be.

- "I'm a super nice person" *(hides behind charm and friendliness, believes the true self is not likable).*
- "Oh, you need help? Ask me!" *(hides behind service to others, disregards their own value and needs as unimportant).*
- "Mr. Smarty-pants" *(hides behind intellect, projecting to have all the answers; covers up a hidden sense of inadequacy).*
- "Mr. Spiritual" *(similar to Mr. Smarty-pants, but far more insidious, as this person hides behind biblical knowledge and piety, covering up for either a lack of awareness that God is after the heart, or covers up the shame they feel in their own hearts).*

Ask God, in His kindness, to reveal which false senses of self you have created in order to project an identity that is not true to who God says you are. As you prayerfully walk through this, allow God to gently expose your shame.

And let me clarify: There is a huge difference between *guilt* and *shame*. Guilt makes you feel bad because you have done something wrong. Shame on the other hand, makes you feel bad because you feel there is something wrong with you. This is an absolutely critical distinction to make, because *shame* is exactly what Jesus came to deal with on the cross (see Hebrews 12).

When we create false selves to cover up our perceived lack of self-value we are essentially telling Jesus that His sacrifice on the cross wasn't really all that worthwhile. Because scripture tells us that we were bought with the very high price of the blood of Jesus[12], and only something incredibly valuable is worth that price. And that "something incredibly valuable" is *you*. It's me. It's all of us.

The lie from the Enemy is that somehow you were the exception and slipped into the divine party uninvited, and that Jesus didn't really want you there and wouldn't have died for you if He really knew you.

---

[12] See 1 Peter 1:18–20.

Throw that lie in the fire because it is absolutely contradictory to scripture. Instead, simply admit to God that you struggle seeing your own value and allow Him to gently show you just how valuable you are to Him.

Remember—the goal is to clear the path for these very questions to get addressed, because God loves us so much and wants to speak life into them. But we first have to acknowledge that these questions exist in order for God to speak into them.

A prayer might look something like this:

> *Dear Jesus, I confess to You now that I have a really hard time seeing my real value. I have created false versions of me that I project for others in the hopes that they might like what they see and that I might be able to hide my truest self from them.*
>
> *Jesus, You promise to cover our shame, exchanging our fig leaves for animal furs, and sacrificing Your very self, Your perfect self, so that we could be known and loved.*
>
> *I receive that now, and ask You to help me see my value in Your eyes.*
>
> *Give me messages of truth to combat the Enemy's schemes in this area, and may I learn to trust Your view of me fully. Help me to discard the false self and instead live out of the 'me' You had in mind when you created the world.*
>
> *Amen.*

A FEW TOOLS TO OFFER

The ways we wrestle control from God and the false selves we put up to hide our truest selves become habitual sins of the heart that take *a lot* of re-training to undo. But the good news is that, as we continually practice making a way for the Lord in our hearts, He will work with us, equipping us to get rid of these rocks in our lives.

Some tools that I've found helpful here are to first *identify* the heart posture that needs adjusting, then *crucify* it, and finally to *sanctify* this area of your heart to God.

IDENTIFY

We need to begin by noticing those areas that our hearts run to that are apart from God. Whether it's a pull for control, another lie you told to protect your persona, or simply a habitual sin of the heart (something you don't necessarily do but notice that the pull of it still carries immense power over you), we start by naming them.

First, list out what it is that you find yourself returning to, time and again. It doesn't have to be "sinful", but simply something that points to a lack of living out of the fullness of God. Maybe you pontificated again in an effort to impress. Maybe you fell back to self-deprecating humor in order to mask your own insecurity. Maybe you dominated a meeting again, filling the room and not letting others provide input, because you wanted to look like the lone hero.

Whatever it is, simply write it down in your journal.

Then the next question, the one that God wants to speak into, is this:

What is my heart running to, beneath the surface, that this sin or desire is trying to answer?

Is your heart running to comfort? Is it seeking belonging? Is your heart trying to escape something? Is it afraid of boredom? Are you seeking security by your own means? Does your heart feel uneasy and is scrambling to find peace?

None of these are abnormal, by the way; these are indications of the human condition. How many stories in the Bible stem from a real person's real struggle with one or more of the above real questions? And how many of God's responses to these real people in the Bible are responses aimed at the heart of the matter?

God cares infinitely more for our hearts than our circumstances, and He will fight fiercely for the former at the expense of the latter. And for that we should be grateful, because when God has our hearts, it is we who benefit immeasurably.

Ok, so after we have worked on identifying our heart questions, we're ready for the next step.

CRUCIFY

> So put to death the sinful, earthly things lurking within you. Have nothing to do with sexual immorality, impurity, lust, and evil desires. Don't be greedy, for a greedy person is an idolater, worshiping the things of this world. Because of these sins, the anger of God is coming. You used to do these things when your life was still part of this world. But now is the time to get rid of anger, rage, malicious behavior, slander, and dirty language. Don't lie to each other, for you have stripped off your old sinful

nature and all its wicked deeds. Put on your new nature, and be renewed as you learn to know your Creator and become like him.

—Colossians 3:5–10 (NLT)

Once we have done the work of identifying those areas that our hearts go to (naming the rocks), we now have to do the tireless work of removing them from our path. The way we do this is by "putting to death" those areas, and replacing them with blessed, renewed hearts. We *identify* the areas of our hearts that need to change, and then we *crucify* them.

When people talk about difficult situations and use the phrase *"Yep, this is just my cross to bear"* I don't think they give full credit to the work Jesus did for us. When Jesus says, "If you want to be my disciple, you must deny yourself, take up your cross daily, and follow me[13]" I don't think He's referring to difficult situations. He's referring to the daily practice of crucifying our sinful nature. And just like anything else that is within one's *nature*, these are deeply ingrained patterns, ways of thinking, and behaviors that, according to Jesus, need to be put to death. *Daily.*

Unfortunately, this concept has turned more into sin management for many of us rather than actual freedom. But according to Galatians, it is *specifically* for the purpose of freedom that Christ has set us free[14].

So how do we balance this paradox: that when Jesus was on the cross, He died for our freedom, but part of that freedom requires that we participate in His death daily.

---

[13] See Luke 9:34.
[14] See Galatians 5:1.

I think rather than moving toward self-flagellation[15] I think what Jesus (and Paul, above) is pointing to is the seriousness with which we must take this directive. Not because we have something to earn, but rather, so much to *gain* if we take this seriously.

Think about the path:

If we fill the valleys, bulldoze the hills, fill in the ruts, but don't remove the rocks, what do we have? Sure we have a path that can be traveled, but the road will have obstacles, setbacks, frustrations, and tripping hazards, whereas if we work hard to remove the rocks, the path can be clear—and with that clear path comes the relief of a smooth journey[16]. One that feels like you and God can travel the road with freedom rather than frustration.

Sadly, I fear that many Christians don't see the value in working to remove the rocks, and so miss out on what God really wants for them. We might clear the rocks on occasion, benefiting from a season of clarity and relational intimacy with God, but then we inadvertently end up putting rocks back on our path, because that's exactly what's in our human nature.

A practice that I have found helpful is simply to ask God where I have rocks in my path. Are there any that I need to be aware of? Have I put any rocks back on the path that we had worked to remove recently? It's an exercise in awareness and also one of approaching God with a heart that says, *I want intimacy with You, and I'm aware*

---

[15] You may not whip yourself physically, but how many of us are brutally unkind to our hearts when it comes to this area?

[16] This "relief of holiness" is a very underrepresented concept and worth spending some mental time on. It's like the relief you have when you're driving the speed limit and later see a highway patrol officer on the side of the road with a radar gun, except exponentially better.

that I am broken and sinful and in my humanity, I return to my old ways—but I want more than that; I want You.

So, the act of crucifying those places in our heart looks like this: paying attention to what is happening in your heart; naming what it is going after in that moment; and then declaring it dead, with Christ's power.

For a concrete example, let's say that I find myself routinely opening up my favorite travel app on my phone and looking for weekend getaways. What starts out as a fairly innocuous desire for a weekend away begins to morph into something that takes up all of my spare time, all of my thoughts, and keeps me awake at night as I ponder the many different options, locations, price points, etc. The questions to ask are, is there anything wrong or overtly sinful about that behavior? Or has the desire for travel become a rock that is in my path that keeps me from experiencing the fullness of God?

How many of us jump on a pattern of behavior, labeling it as unhealthy, without asking the curious questions first? What information would help provide more insight into this "travel bug"? Is my anniversary coming up, and I want to treat my wife to something that is incredibly meaningful to her, and so I comb through the listings because I want to find the perfect place because I care about blessing her with a weekend away and a reminder of how special she is to me? Or are things really difficult at work and I feel like I keep banging my head against a wall, and *I just need to get away from it all for a minute.*

Those scenarios lend clarity, don't they?

And what if, at work, I really do need a reset? And the best way to hit reset is to have a restful and recharging weekend away? Or, what if I have a pattern of regularly running away from the hard stuff, and

I'm really just searching travel sites as a return to my normal mode of escaping when things don't feel successful?

In the first scenario, my heart is for my wife, to celebrate her and to enjoy time with her. In the second, I need a sabbath of sorts, taking a break from the stressors so I can re-engage when I get back and tackle the problems head-on. But in the third, I am resorting to old patterns of avoiding, running, and turning to *escape*.

Maybe in that scenario, what my heart needs more than anything is to actually run *into*, and not *from* the hardship. Maybe a weekend away is a way of conceding defeat, allowing rocks to pile onto the path that could potentially influence other battles I'm fighting as well.

Do you see how critical the heart posture is? Sadly, so many of us just plow through without slowing down and paying attention to what is going on deep inside our hearts.

In the escapism scenario above, crucifying that place in my heart might look something like this:

> *Jesus, I'm noticing that my heart is running toward escape right now. I confess that to You now, and ask that You would give me the courage to engage, and the fortitude to keep fighting for what's good, even though my current circumstances are really difficult.*
>
> *I crucify this part of me that wants to escape, and I am so grateful, Jesus, that when You wanted to escape in Gethsemane, You chose instead to die so that I might also have victory here.*

> *Bring the power of the cross over this area in my heart, Lord, and help me to live in freedom from this.*
>
> *I choose to give my heart to You, Jesus, and not to give in to Escape.*
>
> *Thank you for ministering to me in this place. I love You, Jesus and I choose to engage rather than escape.*
>
> *Thank you for giving me the power to do so; I need it now.*
>
> *In Jesus' name, amen.*

That prayer is a powerful act of crucifying the part in me that wants to escape. It's an act of picking up a rock from the path, tossing it off onto the shoulder of the road, and enjoying the freedom that comes from a clear path to walk with God. And yeah, chances are I'm going to be drawn back to that travel site later today (it's likely become a rut that needs to be filled), and when it does, I can simply say *nope, I'm not going to give my heart back to that right now; Jesus, I give my heart instead to You.*

Do you see the intimacy of this prayer? You are not alone. You don't have to fight your battles alone. With Jesus, we can ask and He will meet us right in our weakness, offering His presence as we reach out to Him.

Do this daily (or more practically, multiple times throughout the day as things come up), and in doing this you are clearing your path, carrying your cross and walking as a true disciple of Jesus.

The good news about the crucifixion is that things didn't end there–for Jesus or for us. Thank God for the resurrection. Our next step, after we put to death (again, daily) those rocks that block our hearts from God, we now get to bring something new, something resurrected, something *sanctified*, over our lives.

SANCTIFY

> Since God chose you to be the holy people he loves, you must clothe yourselves with tenderhearted mercy, kindness, humility, gentleness, and patience. Make allowance for each other's faults, and forgive anyone who offends you. Remember, the Lord forgave you, so you must forgive others. Above all, clothe yourselves with love, which binds us all together in perfect harmony. And let the peace that comes from Christ rule in your hearts. For as members of one body you are called to live in peace. And always be thankful.
>
> Let the message about Christ, in all its richness, fill your lives. Teach and counsel each other with all the wisdom he gives. Sing psalms and hymns and spiritual songs to God with thankful hearts. And whatever you do or say, do it as a representative of the Lord Jesus, giving thanks through him to God the Father.
>
> —Colossians 3:12–17 (NLT)

After we have identified those heart postures that are getting in the way, and after we have crucified them, putting to death the power they have over us, the final step is *sanctification*. Another way to look at this is, after crucifying the sinful places in our hearts, ask *what can be resurrected into something new in that same place?*

WORK TIRELESSLY TO REMOVE THE ROCKS

When we consider Paul's letter to the Colossians, you'll notice he uses very intentional *replacements* from his first list. *Put to death* those things that separate us from God and each other. *Clothe yourself* with those things that are of God.

The verb here refers to an intentionality (I *choose* to get dressed every morning, whether I want to or not) as well a sense of option here (do I want to put on the white shirt or the blue one?) Implicit in the text is this thought that we have some level of action to take every morning in order to put on the character of Christ. In our natural state, we don't have this and will trend toward these sinful patterns, but if we make the conscious decision to replace those with Christ-attributes, we can, in doing so, be imitators of Christ[17].

In fact, when you look at the list of things we're to clothe ourselves with, doesn't it sound like just the type of person you'd love to have as your best friend? Someone who has *tenderhearted mercy. Kindness. Humility. Gentleness. Patience.* Someone who overlooks faults and is *loving and peaceful and filled with gratitude.*

Doesn't that sound like an incredible friend? How would those attributes make your life better? If you were more quick to give allowance for your spouse's faults? If you were kind to everyone, even those who cut you off on the freeway or coworkers who use cutting language directed toward you? If you were patient in how your life is unfolding, allowing time and space for God to do His work in you and in others? If you were humble, and therefore not so offended every time someone fails to recognize your efforts or contributions.

Wouldn't these be incredible?

I believe, through Christ, they are both incredible and attainable.

---

[17] See Ephesians 5.

The key is in sanctifying our hearts and our desires, giving them to Jesus and asking His resurrection power to cover them, transform them, and turn them into something beautiful.

Once you have identified that, by searching those travel sites, your heart is really trying to escape any current challenges you have in your real life, you crucify it:

> *Jesus, I notice that I am running toward escape. I put this desire to death, Lord, and ask that You give me the strength to stay in the moment and face this discomfort head-on.*

And then the sanctification:

> *Jesus, please cover this desire with Your blood. Bring about something new here. Instead of running to escape, may I instead choose Your invitation to holy adventure. I recognize that Your adventure is the best kind, and I surrender my scripted adventures for Your unscripted ones. Give me the strength to face the hardship, and may I experience Your joy as You cover me with your courage and strength, amen.*

Do you see how we are replacing a desire that originates from within with something that comes from God? (Replacing a desire that comes from our sinful nature—our rocks that block the path—and instead covering our own nature with the nature of Christ, removing the rocks and inviting Jesus into that place.)

Our desires can often take the form of seeking comfort, belonging, escape, security, or peace.

If you desire comfort and you are running to alcohol, sex, or Netflix, *ask Jesus to replace these desires with finding comfort in Him.* (It's okay to ask Him what that would look like specifically, if you're unsure.)

If you are seeking belonging, and this search to fill the loneliness and the desire for being included is leading you to look for belonging in all kinds of strange places, *ask Jesus to show you that you belong to Him.* Admit that your heart needs reassurance, and ask Him to give you real reminders that in Him, you are seen and known and loved.

If you are running to escape, *ask Jesus to show you His holy adventure He has for you.*

If you are longing for security and your search for security leads you to put your faith and trust in things that are fickle, illusory, and potentially harmful, *ask Jesus to be the source of your security, reminding you that He has been there since the beginning, asking Him to remind you that He is trustworthy, safe, and good.*

If you are searching for peace, but everywhere you look you see something chaotic and your anxiety spikes because of it, *ask Jesus to be your peace, leading you toward green pastures that restore your soul. Ask Him to fill you with His peace, and offer those places in your heart where anxiety has had too much power over you.*

IN SUMMARY

Our hearts' deepest desire is to be known, seen, and loved, but in our broken humanity we try to fill the voids with things that are temporal and finite. This leads to hills that block the path of our hearts to God, and so we have to work hard to remove those patterns and behaviors that aren't healthy for our relationships—with ourselves, with others, and with God.

Then we examine the habits we have formed over the years and fill the ruts by engaging in spiritual practices that have helped people through the ages connect with God. We read Scripture, we pray, we listen, we create intentional spaces for silence where the noise of this world gets set aside so we can be formed by God. We practice fasting, retreat, and worship.

These practices all bring us into a deeper level of communion with God. And as we do that, we begin to experience being known, seen, and loved. These practices begin to unearth all of the rocks in our path, both above and beneath the surface. They begin to reveal those heart-level issues we need to deal with.

Because God, in His kindness and love, deeply desires to make us whole and holy by His love[18]. But in order to do that, we need to remove those deeper-level things from our lives. We need to get rid of the rocks. If we want to get rid of the rocks that make the path to our hearts bumpy, we have to first name them, then put them to death, then replace them with the character attributes of Jesus.

We identify.

We crucify.

We sanctify.

The key here is in being intentional—daily—about putting on those things that would satisfy our hearts. But we can't do it by ourselves. If that were the case, we would all be experts at sin management; we need the help of Jesus. To take advantage of that help, we work in partnership with Jesus, clearing the path to our hearts, and in receiving that help we are bringing Jesus into our lives in the small details, reminding ourselves that He is Emmanuel. That He is with us.

---

[18] See 1 Thessalonians 5.

WORK TIRELESSLY TO REMOVE THE ROCKS

Now that the path to our hearts is becoming cleared of the clutter and we are experiencing more of Jesus as we are more deeply known, seen, and loved, we get to experience something truly incredible. We get to experience God. Not as we define Him, but as He defines Himself.

As we dive deeper into who God says He is, we also get the incredible benefit of God speaking into who He says we are.

PART TWO
IDENTITY

CHAPTER 7

THE IDENTITY OF GOD

> On hearing his words, some of the people
> said, "Surely this man is the Prophet."
> Others said, "He is the Messiah."
> Still others asked, "How can the Messiah come from Galilee?
> Does not Scripture say that the Messiah will come from
> David's descendants and from Bethlehem, the town where
> David lived?" Thus the people were divided because of Jesus.
>
> —John 7:40–43 (NIV)

> "But what about you?" he asked. "Who do you say I am?"
>
> —Matthew 16:15 (NIV)

"Thus the people were divided because of Jesus."

It's funny. When I talk with people who don't proclaim to follow Jesus, but who instead seem to go with whatever the current social flow of the day is, they all say Jesus was a great teacher, a calm and gentle person, and someone who brought people together. But I rarely hear anyone talk about how divisive Jesus was. He even said it Himself when He made His: *I don't come to unify but to divide* speech[1].

Why don't people nowadays refer to Jesus as a divisive individual? Why instead, the sheep and the lambs and the sitting down in a pasture with flowing robes and people and children crowded around Him? Where is the story, in today's pop culture, of Jesus running around furiously in the temple, making a whip and throwing people out[2]? (In case you weren't quite sure, whipping people and tossing them out would definitely be considered *divisive* actions.)

The problem with most people today as it comes to God and Jesus is the same problem the Pharisees had back when Jesus was face-to-face with them. They have a preconceived notion of who Jesus is, who He isn't, and they try to fit Him into their box.

But Jesus doesn't live in our boxes.

If you read the gospel of John, and in particular chapters 7–10, a strong theme emerges. You have one camp of people who don't believe in Jesus as Messiah, and another who do.

But a deeper look into the story shows a really interesting divide between those who believe and those who don't. Those who believe listen to who Jesus says He is, take His word for it, and follow Him. Those who don't believe get stuck on their preconception of who they thought Messiah would be, and what He would look and act like. So rather than listen to Jesus' claims of who He is, they overlay their own notions of who they think He ought to be; when they compare their ideal Messiah with Jesus, the gap is too wide and so they choose not to believe.

---

[1] See Luke 12:51.
[2] See John 2:13–17.

Doesn't that sound like us sometimes?

If God is good, why is there evil in the world?

If God were real, that wouldn't have happened to me.

If God is love, why do I experience so much hate?

If God is all-powerful, why doesn't He get me out of my current circumstances?

This is natural, but this is also false thinking. It is a product of our fallen humanity. In Eden, the lure was that the fruit would provide a knowledge of good and evil; the lie from the Enemy is that we would be able to tell the difference between the two. We think we know, but remember: our perspective is very limited.

We really don't know.

Let's start by admitting this, because we're all products of Eden. We've all eaten the fruit in one way or another, and as a result we all think we know better. We think we somehow have the right to tell God what He should and shouldn't be doing, what He should and shouldn't allow. But when God doesn't play along with our script, we get angry, we doubt His goodness and perhaps even His existence, and in doing so, we join right in with those Pharisees who had the opportunity to look Jesus in the face and still missed who He was. Simply because there wasn't room in their minds for a God who operated outside their box and so they wouldn't listen. They missed Him.

I don't want us to miss Jesus.

Let's start by simply confessing to God those areas where we've put Him in a box, where we've told Him what He should and shouldn't be doing, and how He can prove His own existence. Let's instead take the posture of those who believed and were saved, and listen to God describe who He is rather than the other way around.

You may have heard it said that God made mankind in His own image, and we've been making God in ours ever since. Let's repent of that posture, and instead humbly sit at the feet of the Almighty, and allow Him to tell us a bit more about Himself:

Back to Isaiah 40:

> Who has scooped up the ocean
> in his two hands,
> or measured the sky between his thumb and little finger,
> Who has put all the earth's dirt in one of his baskets,
> weighed each mountain and hill?
> Who could ever have told GOD what to do
> or taught him his business?
>
> What expert would he have gone to for advice,
> what school would he attend to learn justice?
> What god do you suppose might have taught him what he knows,
> showed him how things work?
> Why, the nations are but a drop in a bucket,
> a mere smudge on a window.
> Watch him sweep up the islands
> like so much dust off the floor!
> There aren't enough trees in Lebanon
> nor enough animals in those vast forests
> to furnish adequate fuel and offerings for his worship.
> All the nations add up to simply nothing before him—
> less than nothing is more like it. A minus.

THE IDENTITY OF GOD

So who even comes close to being like God?
To whom or what can you compare him?
Some no-god idol? Ridiculous!
It's made in a workshop, cast in bronze,
Given a thin veneer of gold,
and draped with silver filigree.
Or, perhaps someone will select a fine wood—
olive wood, say—that won't rot,
Then hire a woodcarver to make a no-god,
giving special care to its base so it won't tip over!

Have you not been paying attention?
Have you not been listening?
Haven't you heard these stories all your life?
Don't you understand the foundation of all things?
God sits high above the round ball of earth.
The people look like mere ants.
He stretches out the skies like a canvas—
yes, like a tent canvas to live under.
He ignores what all the princes say and do.
The rulers of the earth count for nothing.
Princes and rulers don't amount to much.
Like seeds barely rooted, just sprouted,
They shrivel when God blows on them.
Like flecks of chaff, they're gone with the wind.

"So—who is like me?
Who holds a candle to me?" says The Holy.
Look at the night skies:
Who do you think made all this?
Who marches this army of stars out each night,
counts them off, calls each by name
—so magnificent! so powerful!—
and never overlooks a single one?

> Why would you ever complain, O Jacob,
> or, whine, Israel, saying,
> "GOD has lost track of me.
> He doesn't care what happens to me"?
> Don't you know anything? Haven't you been listening?
> GOD doesn't come and go. God *lasts*.
> He's Creator of all you can see or imagine.
> He doesn't get tired out, doesn't pause to catch his breath.
> And he knows *everything*, inside and out.
>
> He energizes those who get tired,
> gives fresh strength to dropouts.
> For even young people tire and drop out,
> young folk in their prime stumble and fall.
> But those who wait upon GOD get fresh strength.
> They spread their wings and soar like eagles,
> They run and don't get tired,
> they walk and don't lag behind.
>
> —Isaiah 40:12–31 (MSG)

When we read things like *"Who is like me?"* and *"who holds a candle to me?"*, it sounds a little bit like the end of the book of Job, doesn't it[3]? God giving us insight into who He is, and also insight into who we aren't.

Volumes upon volumes have been written about the identity of God, so I'm not going to make any feeble attempt at defining God. In

---

[3] If you are unfamiliar, read Job chapters 38–40. It's a big-time smack-down that God lays on Job (in kindness, of course) ending with the statement: "Do you still want to argue with the Almighty? You are God's critic, but do you have the answers?"

fact, I would argue that the very task would be impossible. After all, we've all agreed to acknowledge that God is infinite, right? And remember, Infinite cannot be defined by anything concrete except to acknowledge that *there is always more*, so I won't even bother. However, I do want to offer a *perspective* that I think can be helpful as we seek to understand the identity of God better.

LET GOD SPEAK FOR HIMSELF

The minute you start telling God what to do, repent and surrender your preconceived notions. He is God and you are not. We live in a society that has violated the first commandment, placing ourselves as gods above all others. And when each of us is a god of our own kingdom, the only result is conflict and chaos[4].

So, how do we let God speak for Himself?

We start simply by reading scripture. We practice spiritual disciplines like prayer and fasting. We cut out the noise from our lives and create space for God to speak. We fill the valleys, we bulldoze the hills, we fill the ruts, and we remove the rocks. We clear the path.

When we do that, we create space to experience God as He presents Himself. We remind ourselves that He is who He says He is, and we then get the privilege of experiencing that for ourselves firsthand. It's what makes the whole process worthwhile.

Some other takeaways from Isaiah 40 as God defines Himself:

---

[4] Your kingdom bumps up against mine, mine against yours, ours against others', and it becomes a whole huge mess.

GOD IS POWERFUL OVER NATURE

Ocean, sky, mountains, hills, islands, trees, armies of stars ... (vs. 12–26)

If Elijah prayed that it would not rain and it didn't, and then later he prayed that it would rain and it did[5], maybe that can tell us a bit about the power of God over nature (and quite a bit about the power of prayer from a righteous person as well.) After all, if God created nature, He can certainly manipulate it to serve His greater purpose. If Jesus can walk on water, I'm going to go ahead and state that the very act demonstrates some measure of authority over the elements.

While we participate in caring for nature (something God placed on us from the beginning, by the way), we also acknowledge that He is sovereign over the wind, sky, temperature, rain, snow, sun, and the stars–all of it. This does not give us a free pass to abuse His creation, but rather sets us in a position to be submissive to it, respect it, pray for it, and care for it.

But at the end of the day we are not the ones *in control* of global warming. We have an incredibly strong *influence*, but not control. We are not in control of ice caps or of endangered penguins–we have been given a role in participating in the earth's stewardship, but the ultimate outcome is not ours; that belongs to God exclusively[6].

---

[5] See 1 Kings 18–19.

[6] I realize I may have lost half of you just now. I'm not making a political statement but rather a theological one. One that states that God has given us an incredible responsibility and influence to be good stewards of His creation. And many good arguments can be made that we've not held up our end of that responsibility. However–we need to be very careful that our efforts are kept within the perspective that, in spite of our best efforts, we are not God. We can (and should) be good stewards of Creation. But only God (and God alone) can *control* it.

GOD IS POWERFUL OVER GOVERNMENTS

The nations are a drop in a bucket, they add up to nothing before him (vs. 16–17); he ignores the princes and what they say and do, the rulers count for nothing (vs. 23–24)

This should come as an incredible relief, unless you're sitting under an oppressive government, in which case it will potentially cause incredible doubt and confusion.

Just remember that God is in control. He is in control of who ultimately sits in office during any given period of time. He is in control of whomever has influence over global leaders. He is in control of all outcomes politically.

He is also a staunch supporter of free will (He created it, after all), and so the further and further we get from God, the more He allows us to face the consequences (good and bad) of our choices.

If we seem like we're stuck in a rudderless society, let's recall Elijah's prayer for rain and how powerful that was, and let's focus those prayers on our leaders—that they might be surrounded by people who fear God and surround themselves with others who point them in the direction of the Almighty.

If God is sovereign even over world governments, He is not surprised if and when they act unstable, whether or not they go to war, or how great or how badly they treat their people. God is not surprised by any of it. And we can trust that, because as we are in the habit of practicing daily communion with Him, He has us and will protect us regardless of what any outside circumstances might suggest.

A great study to underscore this would be to read through the book of Acts. While the local political powers were set in opposition to the Church, and while external circumstances seemed to indicate that there was no hope for God's people at all, He actually used persecution of the Church as a way to rapidly and effectively spread the gospel.

It's a good reminder that in life, there are always two story arcs at play: what we see with our eyes, and what God is up to in peoples' hearts.

Keeping that in perspective will yield much peace in our lives.

GOD IS POWERFUL OVER _____

Nobody even comes close ... (vs. 18); God is above it all ... (vs. 21–22) If God is powerful over nature, and if He is powerful over governments, then He is also powerful over *anything* that you might be facing right now. Because we trust that He is good and loving, and that He is constantly working things out for the good of those who love Him[7], we can also trust that whatever we're up against right now, He has already overcome. He may choose to allow us to suffer rather than give us an escape hatch, but this too is part of the "working all things for good". After all, God is most interested in our character development and sometimes, painful though they may be at the time, difficult circumstances are the best teacher.

When you're faced with these types of situations, a great place to begin is to simply ask God a couple of questions:

> *Are there any valleys, hills, ruts, or rocks that I need to be aware of that this situation is revealing so I can grow?*
>
> *Is there anything I'm missing here, Lord?*

---

[7] See Romans 8:28.

> *Will you help me to experience Your presence with me in this suffering, Jesus?*

These help us maintain a heart posture that recognizes that Jesus is Emmanuel, admits that God is in control and we are not, and invites intimacy with God through the process.

Sometimes there are blessings in the suffering; we just need to ask God to show us where those are.

GOD IS NURTURING

He energizes those who get tired, gives fresh strength to dropouts. (vs. 30)

I think people tend to generally fit God into one of two camps: God is all-powerful and therefore should wave His mighty hand and make the world's problems disappear, or God is the supreme Nurturer and therefore never would confront anyone on what might be labeled as "sin". The truth is, if we take the approach where we let God speak for Himself, then we have to agree that He is both.

I think Jesus' response to the woman caught in adultery models this well: Jesus, being all-powerful and yet incredibly nurturing, writes something in the dirt with his fingers—something that, according to Scripture, was enough to start sending the accusers away, beginning with the oldest[8]. Some have speculated that Jesus was writing the sins each of the bystanders had committed; others have suggested that He was writing the names of the other dudes she had slept with—guys that were very potentially present to watch what Jesus was doing.

---

[8] See John 8:1–11.

The content remains a mystery, but the point remains: Whatever Jesus wrote was enough to drive the accusers away. It must have held some kind of insight and power, otherwise they would have likely concluded that He was ignoring them and gone about their business of stoning the girl.

While Jesus was all-powerful (and all-knowing) with the accusers, he was unbelievably tender and compassionate to the woman who was caught. And in that tenderness and compassion, Jesus wasn't just *nice*, He was after something greater: He was after restoring her dignity. I think that's why many speculate that Jesus was writing down the sexual sins of her accusers in the dirt; it was a way of leveling the playing field and letting everyone know that we're all broken, none of us is perfect, so let's give this poor lady a break, shall we?

There are countless other stories in Scripture that point to God's nurturing heart: Ishmael and Hagar; Elijah after running from Jezebel; most of the Psalms; the life and ministry of Jesus, and so on.

Scripture is filled with God as nurturer.

But when we take a stance on which aspect of the "all-powerful" vs. "nurturing" scale God is supposed to be operating on in any given circumstance, we put on the Pharisee outfit—we take another bite of the fruit, thinking we know what's good and what's evil; and worse, we judge God.

Let's instead, with humility, embrace the mystery of a finger drawing in the dirt, a woman's dignity restored; a God who can decide for Himself when He wants to smite and when He wants to embrace.

GOD DOESN'T ABANDON US

Why would you whine, saying "God has lost track of me. He doesn't care what happens to me?" God doesn't come and go. God lasts. (vs. 27)

It's interesting to note how many times we as humans feel abandoned by God. David wrote about it in the Psalms, Jesus Himself echoed that from the cross[9]. I know many good disciples of Jesus who, in the context of following God, have still felt abandoned by Him. I wonder if this is just part of the Christian journey. Because if the saints have felt abandoned, why should we be surprised when we do as well?

I will say from personal experience that in times where I have felt abandoned by God, later (sometimes much later) and through much prayer and reflection, I have seen that God was there even when I couldn't see Him.

One of my favorite stories is when Elijah has a serious smack-down on Mt. Carmel. He challenges the prophets of Baal in a "God vs. god" showdown for the ages. Of course, God is glorified, and the god Baal is shown for what he is–an imposter god. Elijah then follows that up with a massacre of the prophets of Baal (yeah, the Bible can get gory at times), and then prays earnestly for rain to come and relieve the land from its drought. God answers, and rain comes to cover the land[10].

By any standards, this would have been a pretty epic day. Imagine: You burn with zeal for God Almighty, you are at odds with the prophets of a false god who has led your people astray; you challenge them to a showdown so you can reveal how powerful the God you serve is. You win the showdown, big-time, even though you

---

[9] See Matthew 27:46, where Jesus quotes Psalm 22 as he hangs on the cross.
[10] For this incredible story, see 1 Kings 18–19.

intentionally stack the deck against yourself[11]. You then spend some real time in serious prayer, and you change the weather, ending a long-standing drought that has lasted for years. A pretty good day, wouldn't you say?

But does Elijah celebrate? Not really, because he learns that Jezebel, a powerful ruler, has vowed to take his life by the next morning. So Elijah runs. And he runs really, really fast[12].

He outruns Jezebel, and we are told, "he came to a broom bush, sat down under it and prayed that he might die. "I have had enough, Lord," he said. "Take my life; I am no better than my ancestors." Then he lay down under the bush and fell asleep[13]." An angel comes and gives him food (good call–how many of us throw "hangry tantrums"?) and lets him rest. After another meal and a nap, God invites Elijah to encounter Him–after 40 days of running in hiding from Jezebel.

Now, when we read this story, the *40 days* thing is just a line in a sentence. But imagine what must have been going through Elijah's mind as he ran for his life for over a month. I'm guessing he wasn't feeling super close to God over the course of those few weeks. Maybe he was, but if it were me, I would be feeling alone (because he was), abandoned (even though we find out later that he wasn't) and completely destitute (he was running for his life, after all). I would be crying out to God, wondering where He was, why He had forsaken me, and why He was content leaving me in the wilderness to die.

---

[11] Again, read the story for yourself, but Elijah has them throw buckets and buckets of water on his sacrifice, and God lights it up anyways. It's pretty epic.
[12] Although I am seriously jealous of this dude's speed and endurance, I wonder how many times I've run hard and fast away from situations, based on fear. How quickly we forget the God-victories in the face of adversity. At least I know I'm not alone in my human forgetfulness of God's victories…
[13] 1 Kings 19:4b–5a.

In fact, I have done these very things. And while not wandering a physical desert, I have experienced the dryness of my own internal emotional and spiritual desert; that feeling that comes when you wonder where God is, how He, in His all-powerful state hasn't changed your circumstances, and you crave, at a heart level, the nurturing presence of God Almighty.

It's a terrible place to be.

And it seems like this is not an unfamiliar place for most of God's people. So if you are feeling alone, if you feel abandoned by God, and you feel like you've done everything you know to do and He still feels distant, keep on hanging on. Because if Elijah can come straight from a major victory to the throes of despair and death, then maybe his story can further encourage us:

> And the word of the Lord came to him: "What are you doing here, Elijah?"
>
> He replied, "I have been very zealous for the Lord God Almighty. The Israelites have rejected your covenant, torn down your altars, and put your prophets to death with the sword. I am the only one left, and now they are trying to kill me too."
>
> —1 Kings 19:9b–10 (NIV)

Do you know what's so beautiful here? Elijah, after running for 40 days, is approached by God. *God comes after him.*

And do you notice the gentleness in His question? There is no judgment, no accusation, just a simple and tender question. In fact, I'm not quite sure where *here* is, but I wonder if it was someplace familiar to Elijah. Maybe it was a place from his old life, perhaps before he started serving God. Like Peter returning to fishing after the crucifixion[14], like so many of us returning to what's familiar when we feel God has left us, we get this tender, gentle question: *What are you doing here?*

If you feel abandoned by God, what if He were to ask you that right now? How would you respond?

I love the honesty of Elijah's response: *Hey Lord, I've been doing your work, serving you faithfully, and where has it led me? I'm running for my life and I'm all alone in this fight. This is my reward??*

Let's look at God's response. Notice He doesn't answer Elijah's question right away:

> The Lord said, "Go out and stand on the mountain in the presence of the Lord, for the Lord is about to pass by."
>
> Then a great and powerful wind tore the mountains apart and shattered the rocks before the Lord, but the Lord was not in the wind. After the wind there was an earthquake, but the Lord was not in the earthquake. After the earthquake came a fire, but the Lord was not in the fire. And after the fire came a gentle whisper. When Elijah heard it, he pulled his cloak over his face and went out and stood at the mouth of the cave.
>
> Then a voice said to him, "What are you doing here, Elijah?"
>
> —1 Kings 19:11–13 (NIV)

---

[14] See John 21.

Notice what happens here. Rather than answer him right away, God *invites* Elijah to *experience* Him. And have you noticed how Elijah experiences God? *A gentle whisper.*

It's almost as though God needed to help Elijah clear the path to his heart through 40 days of running, and through wind, through an earthquake, and through a fire, so that after the path was clear and uncluttered, Elijah could be in a spot where he could hear the whisper of God.

It's so incredibly beautiful.

If you feel abandoned by God, don't give up hope. He may feel distant, but He is a God who pursues—both our hearts and *us*. When He comes (He is God, after all, and His timing is not ours), make sure to keep the path to your heart clear—no valleys, no hills, no ruts, and no rocks. Because when He comes, it may very well be through a gentle whisper and your heart will be oh so refreshed to hear it.

Now that Elijah is tuned in, let's see how God answers:

> Then a voice said to him, "What are you doing here, Elijah?"
>
> He replied, "I have been very zealous for the Lord God Almighty. The Israelites have rejected your covenant, torn down your altars, and put your prophets to death with the sword. I am the only one left, and now they are trying to kill me too."
>
> The Lord said to him, "Go back the way you came, and go to the Desert of Damascus. When you get there, anoint Hazael king over Aram. Also, anoint Jehu son of Nimshi king over Israel, and

anoint Elisha son of Shaphat from Abel Meholah to succeed you as prophet. Jehu will put to death any who escape the sword of Hazael, and Elisha will put to death any who escape the sword of Jehu. Yet I reserve seven thousand in Israel—all whose knees have not bowed down to Baal and whose mouths have not kissed him."

—1 Kings 19:13–18 (NIV)

God asks the same question as before; Elijah responds the same way. But this time, God gives Elijah some specific instructions on what he is to do. And then He drops something incredible: *I have seven thousand others who have not given in to the pressures of the local culture.* In other words:

You are not alone.

Even though Elijah felt alone, abandoned, and destitute for 40 long and lonely days, God had other information that Elijah was not aware of. Even though he felt like he was the only one who was fighting for the one and only God, God had others who were fighting the same battles.

Elijah was not alone. And neither are you, even if you find yourself wandering in an emotional or spiritual desert. Keep seeking God's presence; keep clearing your path, so that when that gentle whisper comes, you are ready for it. And when it comes, may the God of peace fill your heart with His presence, filling your soul as you come to know that God is with you. He will never leave you. He will never abandon you.

And as Isaiah points out in the beginning of Chapter 40, may you find *comfort* in that knowledge.

GOD HAS BEEN THERE SINCE THE BEGINNING AND WILL BE THERE THROUGH THE END

God doesn't come and go. God lasts. He's Creator of all you can see or imagine. He doesn't get tired out, doesn't pause to catch his breath. (vs. 28)

In a world where almost everything seems transitory, isn't it reassuring to know that God simply *exists*? Think about it: Our technology is built for obsolescence–your new phone is designed to be obsolete in two years so that you'll be motivated to buy a new one and keep the money flowing. Social trends are obsolete almost as soon as they're popular. Even nations come and go[15].

But God lasts. And isn't that reassuring? I know–some people out there think that God is old (or at least outdated and old-fashioned). I mean, if you've been around since the beginning, I suppose "old" isn't inappropriate. But the people who call God old tend to be the same ones who dismiss Him as antiquated and irrelevant.

Those people likely haven't read the Bible. If they did, they would see that really not much has changed in human nature since the very beginning.

We all want to be our own gods, and so to preserve our own kingdoms we kill, we slander, we steal, we hate, we ignore, we condescend, we compare, we judge; we do all kinds of terrible things to one another. All because we try to play God. And I know, those same people will point out the good things about humanity: We feed the hungry, we put people through medical school so they can heal the sick, we help our neighbor, we smile at the cashier at the grocery store, we spread a little love and kindness wherever we go. And while these good

---

[15] I remember learning the geography of all of the countries in Africa during a college class, only to now feel totally inept as I help my children with their World History just a few decades later.

things may be true, I think an honest look into one's own heart will reveal that both the good aspects and the bad aspects are very likely true at the same time.

In fact, if someone isn't able to see the darkness (sin) in his or her heart, that is a very dangerous spot. I've been there, and it was about as far from God as I've ever been—all under the guise that I was a good person doing good things.

So, if *God isn't outdated*, (this is confirmed as we recognize that His story of humanity is just as true then as it is now, and that He has been with us—humanity—since the very beginning) then we can trust that *His presence will be with us* (if we allow it) into the future as well.

In fact, Jesus Himself said that He would be with us always, *even to the end of the age*[16]. There ought to be something incredibly reassuring about the eternal nature of Emmanuel. Not only will He not abandon us, but He won't abandon us ... *ever*. And *ever* means even after you die; He won't abandon your children or your grandchildren—He will be with us to the very end of the age.

An infinite God is a God worthy of our worship and our hearts' devotion. And this infinite God promises to be steadfast, holy, and *there* for us. He always has been, He always is, and He always will be.

Amen to that.

GOD GIVES US STRENGTH

But those who wait upon God will get fresh strength. They spread their wings and soar like eagles, they run and don't get tired, they walk and don't lag behind. (vs. 31)

---

[16] See Matthew 28:20.

God gives His people strength. *If and when* they wait upon Him. And isn't that "waiting upon Him" just the worst?

I for one am an impatient person. I've experienced growth in this particular area, where I mostly don't yell at other cars while I'm driving down the road, unless of course, they're being erratic, and now I just talk under my breath to them.

I call it progress.

You would think that a lifetime of driving in Southern California would have developed my patience, but no, it simply *tests* it. Day after day after day. And though I often fail those tests, I really have grown in my ability to be patient. If you don't believe me, just ask. But please ask in an efficient manner so we can get to the point right away, because I don't really want to wait an eternity for you to get the question out. Cool?

But seriously, God has grown this area in my life. One of the ways He's done this is a simple phrase when things aren't going according to my grand script: *"I don't prefer it*[17]*"*. Saying *I don't prefer the traffic* or *I don't prefer the scorching heat* or *I don't prefer how long the DMV is taking to process this incredibly simple form* has really done wonders. That simple phrase removes the power of circumstantial situations over me. The traffic no longer has power over my emotional well-being. With a simple *I don't prefer it*, now I'm suddenly the one with power over my emotions. When a driver acts like an utter maniac and endangers himself and others, and I simply utter *I don't prefer his driving style*, I can now laugh at him and at myself.

So what does this have to do with patience?

---

[17] A huge thank-you to my good friend, Dan Crowley, for teaching me this incredibly valuable phrase.

When an external situation no longer has power over me, I am now able to be more relaxed in the midst of it. And when I'm more relaxed in that situation, I am more willing to wait. And when I'm more willing to wait, I am exhibiting patience. So when God is taking longer to answer my question than I would like, instead of sinking into the depths of despair, I can now calmly say *I don't prefer having to wait on God like this.* That calmness actually maintains a clear path for God to meet me there; for Him to give me fresh strength.

Years ago, I used to be a high school teacher. I taught at my alma mater and used to make Hotel California jokes to the parents during Back to School Night (you know, *you can check out but you can never leave*–that's how I felt about my high school). I sensed God calling me into something different and began making arrangements to transition out of my teaching career. Throughout that season, I had many hardships, a few highs, several lows, and then I was finally able to leave teaching.

Seven years later.

I didn't prefer that.

But you know what? During that span, I learned all kinds of things about God. And I learned all kinds of things about myself. I learned how to be content in circumstances even when they weren't of my choosing. I learned how to be faithful to my job, teaching my students well, even though I knew I was on my way out. I learned how to cry out, "How long, Oh Lord!" like the Psalmist[18]. I learned how to manage my anxiety every fall as a new school year would begin. I learned how to lean on God for daily strength to fight through the resistance and the obstacles. I learned the value of praying for my students before they got into the classroom. I learned the value of good friendships and a supportive wife when things weren't going

---

[18] Psalm 40 became my personal anthem for several years.

so well at work. And when the door opened for a different career opportunity, I also learned that God's timing really was best, even though it didn't fit my script. The waiting made it so abundantly clear that the timing was God's, that He was in it, and that it was the right move to make.

All of that patient endurance, all of those *I don't prefer this*, all of the prayers, gave me fresh strength. It gave me a closeness with God, even in the challenges, even when the script wasn't how I would have written it, even when I didn't agree with God's timing. Leaning on Him (daily) showed me that I can grow through hardship; it showed me that God is faithful during hardship; and it showed me that ultimately, He can be trusted even when I don't quite know what's going on.

God gives us strength when we wait on him.

It's one of the most difficult things to do, but like the view after a strenuous hike, it carries incredible rewards. And you know one of the best rewards? Knowing Him as He reveals Himself, and deconstructing our own preconceived notions of who He is. Being known by Him as we receive more of Him through our clear path to the heart. Those results bring about the ultimate desire of our true hearts.

They bring about closeness with God.

CHAPTER 8

YOUR TRUE IDENTITY

When Friedrich Nietzche wrote that "God is dead" back in 1882, he didn't necessarily see this as a good thing[1]. And while many vilify Nietzche for saying what he said, I believe it was simply an observation of a post-Enlightenment culture–a culture that had deemed philosophy and science as sovereign, and therefore had rejected its need for God.

Funny how "enlightenment" works, isn't it? Rather than see Jesus as the light of the world[2], we see the sciences as the true enlightenment. Rather than place our trust in a sovereign, all-powerful and all-knowing God, we instead "trust the science".

Now, before I lose half of you, let me say outright that my educational background was in the sciences[3]. I studied through the University

---

[1] He wrote in *Twilight of the Idols*: "When one gives up the Christian faith, one pulls the right to Christian morality out from under one's feet. This morality is by no means self-evident... Christianity is a system, a whole view of things thought out together. By breaking one main concept out of it, the faith in God, one breaks the whole." While I don't necessarily agree with his assessment of Christianity, he is astute to note that we lose our entire foundation when we lose God.
[2] John 8:12.
[3] I got my degrees Mathematics and Mechanical Engineering at UCSD.

of California system, so please don't label me as "just another science-hating Christian who puts his brain on the shelf in favor of a blind and ignorant faith".

I'd prefer to think of it as an exercise in using the Scientific Method and critical observation as I work to love God with all of my mind, observing scripture and how it interacts with the world around us. And what I observe, when I look at our world, is a culture who has set God on the shelf, leaning instead on our own understanding[4] as we seek to carve our own path rather than clear the one God has laid out for us. In fact, for most people, the only time they take God off the shelf to dust Him off is when they need someone to blame for their misery and misfortune. And that is a true tragedy.

As a society we have moved beyond the Pharisaical approach of trying to put God in our box, and instead divorced ourselves from Him completely.

The result?

Simply look around and notice how determined (yet directionless) we are; how fiercely devoted (to ourselves) we are; how quick to be good (while rejecting holiness) we are; and how dependent on the validation from others (but sadly, not God) we are.

It's this last point—this dependence on others for validation—that I think shows up so clearly in our society. Scroll through your favorite social media platform and simply ask yourself if these people seem secure in who they are. Don't ask it with judgment, but rather, ask with compassion. Better yet, remove yourself from the exercise and imagine if Jesus were scrolling through; how would He react? With anger? With disgust? Or would He look upon our posts with

---

[4] In direct contrast to Proverbs 3:5–6.

compassion, recognizing that we are sheep without a shepherd[5]? The tragic thing is, as a society we have bought into the notion that we are the shepherds of our lives.

Talk about blindness.

While I'm not trying to disparage social media, I am merely trying to point out that it can be incredibly informative of where we are as a society.

We self-proclaim.

We self-promote.

We self-identify.

We self-express.

Why? Because in a world where God is dead, that leaves only us left as the ones able to confirm that others are seen and known and loved. And as I've argued earlier, the finite will *never* be a long-term substitute for the Infinite.

But in a God-oriented paradigm, we can reframe the whole situation. Rather than us being in charge of ourselves (which is an immense amount of pressure, by the way), let's settle into the idea that we have the option to be partners with God as He guides and directs us.

Does that lessen your anxiety a bit?

How can we best partner with God and be confident that it is He who is guiding us and not ourselves or our societal influences? We make a daily habit of clearing the path. Filling the valleys, moving

---

[5] See Matthew 9:36.

the hills, filling the ruts, and clearing out the rocks. We do this in community with others who recognize the vitality of this as well, and we spur each other on in our walks with Jesus. Because only Jesus can truly speak to the core of who we are. Only Jesus can convince us that, even in our most raw of places, we are *seen*, we are *known*, and we are *loved*. And from this place, we can rest in our identity in Him, bringing God back to the center of our lives, orienting ourselves within the context of God's structure and order–because after all, if we take Him for who He says He is, He truly wants what's best for us.

But we also recognize that our finite perspective is limited and we don't always have the clearest of pictures of what is best, and so we consciously surrender that to God, trusting in Him as He guides, directs, sees, knows, and loves us.

And with this approach, God is anything but dead.

GOD IS CENTRAL

Now that we've (hopefully) brought God back into the center of our worldview, let's remind ourselves of a few key facts:

God is God, and we are not[6].

He is powerful over nature (we are not).

He is powerful over governments (we are not).

---

[6] Back to the 1st Commandment. I am convinced that God put this first, because if we all got that one right, we wouldn't really need the other nine, right? (Before you cry anathema, just ponder that for a while and see how it lands–what would our world look like if we all, collectively, put God *first*?)

He is powerful over diseases (we are not).

Continuing within that framework, God is sovereign and we are not. God knows more than we do—about ourselves, about our world, and about humanity in general. God created the world, we did not.

In fact, if you look at every technological advancement (for ease, let's just take every advancement from the Enlightenment to present day), they all are geared toward one of three categories:

- *Man vs. Nature* (think air conditioning, modern transportation, even umbrellas).
- *Man vs. Man* (modern weaponry, locks on our doors, even football pads).
- *Man vs. God* (gender reassignment surgeries, bioengineering, even hair coloring).

And while I personally am SO grateful for air conditioning, air travel, and Air Jordans, it's worth noting the potential effects on our souls as we enjoy these wonderful technological advancements:

I am no longer subject to the conditions and constraints of Nature.

Too hot? Turn on the a/c.

Too cold? Flip the switch to heater mode.

Too rainy? Go inside.

To dry? Pull out the humidifier.

How about Man vs. Man?

If I have the best technology, I am no longer subject to the control of others.

In a rather grisly example, if I stake my claim on a particular piece of land, and someone comes to try to take it from me, I have the technology to load a gun, shoot them and remove the threat they pose to my property. Gather enough like-minded folks, and collectively we can all lay claim to a cluster of adjacent properties and defend them with weaponry. Over time, those inside that collection of like-minded people will gather and form hierarchies of leadership, and likely those will be the ones with the best technology so they can remain in power.

And finally, Man vs. God.

With the right technology, I am no longer subject to an Outside determinant—of my gender, my biology, even certain aspects of my personality.

Again–my aim here is not to bash technology nor is it to suggest that we would be better off without it. My aim is simply to identify the current waters we're swimming in so that we can be aware of their effects on us. And one of the most poignant effects of modern technology is that it gives us the illusion that we are the ones who are in control and that we don't have to submit to or be subject to anything (or anyone) else.

The message is that we control our destiny and we control how to get there. In other words, we have eaten the fruit, we have metabolized it, and its effects work their way through our very core. We are like gods. And if we're honest, that is a lot of pressure. Because people weren't designed to be gods. Only God has what it takes to carry that burden.

So while technology has provided innumerable benefits to society, we would be wise to pay attention to the condition of our own souls, and we would be strategic to practice tangible exercises that remind us that we are not ultimately the ones in control. Taking a leisurely walk without listening to music or a podcast focuses my attention on the conditions around me: the temperature, the breeze, the birds— whether these are pleasing to me or not, I notice them, and I notice that I am subject to these elements; they are not subject to me.

Unplugging from technology for an afternoon reminds me that the world goes on without me, and that the news, events, or social posts that I think are so important for my well-being really aren't that important at all.

Tent camping reminds me that I am subject to something much bigger than myself. I have no control over the temperature, over when the sun rises and when it sets, and let's face it—I also have no control over when the air mattress is going to lose its will, allowing my hips to rest not-so-gently on the hard rocks below, reminding me that I am a fragile being who is only getting more and more subject to his age.

Or am I the only one who has those experiences while camping?

The point is, despite what most everything around us seems to indicate, we aren't really in control of very much. And at a heart level, that actually should provide a measure of relief. Because if we aren't in control, then we aren't actually gods. And if we aren't gods, then we don't have the pressure to be God Himself. And if we don't have the pressure to be God, then we can let Him be God, and we can rest in that position; we can trust that God is good, because we have cleared the path to our hearts and learned to take Him at His word on this.

That puts God back in center position in our hearts. At least for now. Then, in our frail human nature, our peaceful, easy feeling with God at the center will last approximately thirty seconds before it is stolen away by some new worry or care that edges its way in. (While I jest about the thirty seconds, it's actually more true than we want to admit.)

Like any form of exercise, when those worries creep back in, we just need to practice putting God back in the center. After a while, those thirty seconds become sixty, then they become ninety seconds, then five minutes, then ten, and so on until you have an entire morning where you rest in the assurance that God is in control of everything. And if He is in control of everything, then He can also speak into the very place of our hearts that often contains the most questions: *Our Identity*.

GOD GIVES US OUR IDENTITY

The most tragic thing about our current culture is that we have divorced ourselves from God. We take on all the pressure that comes with being divine, and as we've seen in the previous chapter, only the Divine truly has the right to self-proclaim. The rest of us would benefit from a little humility as we realize this important aspect of where we stand relative to God.

But when we, as a society, remove God from the center, then the duty to proclaim our identity falls on us. And because we are fickle people, our sense of identity is often a moving target, influenced and affirmed (or rejected) by the people around us. Sounds like an incredible amount of power to give away, doesn't it?

Our current social moment as it relates to identity assumes that we, as individuals, have all the power. But if we're constantly requiring affirmation from *others*, then who actually has the power in the situation? (Insert mic drop here.)

YOUR TRUE IDENTITY

The effects of a self-proclaiming society are many, but one worth highlighting is simply that it is remarkably unstable. If you're not convinced, just spend an hour scrolling through the news and ask yourself if the stories reflect a stable, secure society or not. Actually, don't spend an hour; it might very likely sink you into clinical depression, and nobody wants that. How many people in our culture are woefully insecure[7]? How many of *us*, even as Christ-followers, are woefully insecure?

So, allow me to propose a way out, and this is a critical philosophical shift. The objective, from the very beginning, was that God would be the One to proclaim identity, not us.

Yes, He gave us the assignment of giving names to animals, but He was the one who named Adam, who named Eve, and who established their identities. He spoke; He declared. And it was.

> Then God said, "Let us make mankind in our image, in our likeness, so that they may rule over the fish in the sea and the birds in the sky, over the livestock and all the wild animals, and over all the creatures that move along the ground."
>
> So God created mankind in his own image,
> in the image of God he created them;
> male and female he created them.

---

[7] Scroll through any social media platform and tell me that it's overrun with people who are remarkably grounded in who they are. And while you may find a few exceptions, the majority are seeking affirmation, likes and shares, and therefore validation from those in their network. And before you are too critical here, let's at least be honest and admit that you and I do the exact same thing whenever we post anything.

> God blessed them and said to them, "Be fruitful and increase in number; fill the earth and subdue it. Rule over the fish in the sea and the birds in the sky and over every living creature that moves on the ground."
>
> —Genesis 1:26–28 (NIV)

Remember: This story happens in Eden; this is what God called *good*.

God created us in His image, speaks to us, gives us names, and gives us assignment and purpose, which provides meaning. By doing this, *He gives us our very identities.*

Let that sink in for a moment.

In God's system, one where He gives us our identity, this translates into assignment, into meaning, and into purpose. And how many of us right now are struggling to find meaning and purpose in our lives? How many of us just want to be told what to do, to have our *assignment* handed to us so we can have direction and fulfillment, meaning and purpose? How many books, lectures and philosophical debates have been about the *purpose or meaning of life*?

I believe God, in His original plan, designed Himself to be the One who gives us those things. But in our divorced-from-God culture, we have determined that it is up to *us* to be the ones to determine our purpose and our meaning. How has that worked out so far? People feel directionless, so they change cities, change careers, change spouses. People feel that they have no purpose, so they sink into depression, anxiety, and despair, wondering if anyone would even notice if they were gone or if they died. People struggle with finding meaning, so they opt for meaningless activities or substances that numb the soul, because facing reality is too painful.

We don't have to live that way.

We can live lives of meaning and purpose and identity–we just have to stop trying so hard to self-define these things, and instead learn to listen to the voice of God who is the only One who can truly speak to these areas in our souls.

So how do we actually *do* this? How do we actually start to make the shift so we can experience meaning and purpose as it stems out of our identity? It first starts with making a *daily discipline* of clearing the path to our hearts. We identify, crucify, and sanctify those areas where we have placed obstacles in the way.

By doing this we are reminded that God is central and we are not.

And we rest in this reality, because when the path to our heart is clear, and we keep God central, we are remembering Eden and the shalom of God. From this place, we allow God to speak; we give Him space to proclaim our identity, and then we *rest* in that identity.

Isn't there a place in your heart that just craves this right now?

Here's how we do this (and I really recommend slowing *way down* and engaging with this, even if it takes some time):

INVITE GOD INTO THE PROCESS

Grab your journal, find a quiet place, and start with prayer:

> *Jesus, I surrender everything to You right now—every person, every object, every dream, every worry. I ask that You would fill me with Your presence right now; may I feel Your peace over me in this place.*

> *Lord Jesus, please show me any remaining valleys, hills, ruts, or rocks that I might need to deal with in my heart. I crucify these, and I ask that You would sanctify these areas of my heart.*
>
> *I set aside any notions of my false self and put those on the side of the path too, Lord, so that You and I might have a deeper communion together right now.*
>
> *I also lay aside anything that I run to for comfort or for significance, and I simply choose to sit here, with You, in this moment.*
>
> *Jesus, I ask that You would speak to my identity now. Who do You say I am? I confess there are many times where I self-proclaim, and I lay that at Your feet now; I open myself up to You and Your words over my life.*
>
> *I ask, again, that You would speak to me, Jesus. Amen.*

Now, in this tender space, let's look at some of the things God says about us:

> For we know that our old self was crucified with him so that the body ruled by sin might be done away with, that we should no longer be slaves to sin. (Romans 6:6)

> See what great love the Father has lavished on us, that we should be called children of God! And that is what we are! The reason the world does not know us is that it did not know him. Dear friends, now we are children of God, and what we will be has not yet been made known. But we know that when Christ

appears, we shall be like him, for we shall see him as he is. (1 John 3:1–2)

But you are a chosen people, a royal priesthood, a holy nation, God's special possession, that you may declare the praises of him who called you out of darkness into his wonderful light. (1 Peter 2:9)

Since, then, you have been raised with Christ, set your hearts on things above, where Christ is, seated at the right hand of God. Set your minds on things above, not on earthly things. For you died, and your life is now hidden with Christ in God. (Colossians 3:1–3)

I have been crucified with Christ. It is no longer I who live, but Christ who lives in me. And the life I now live in the flesh I life by faith in the Son of God, who loved me and gave himself for me. (Galatians 2:20)

In him we have redemption through his blood, the forgiveness of our trespasses, according to the riches of his grace… (Ephesians 1:7)

I praise you, for I am fearfully and wonderfully made. Wonderful are your works; my soul knows it very well. (Psalm 139:14)

For at one time you were darkness, but now you are light in the Lord. Walk as children of light. (Ephesians 5:8)

Who saved us and called us to a holy calling, not because of our works but because of his own purpose

> and grace, which he gave us in Christ Jesus before the ages began... (2 Timothy 1:9)
>
> For we know, brothers loved by God, that he has chosen you... (1 Thessalonians 1:4)

Go back and read those as often as you need to. The goal is communion with Jesus. If anything stirs in you as you read, pause and reflect on what it was that moved you. Invite Jesus into the process.

Then, in your journal, ask Jesus if there is anything else He would like to say to you. Prayerfully walk through this; reject any accusations and test everything through scripture, but write down what He offers you. It could be something simple like:

- "I am a child of God."
- "I am God's beloved."
- "I am fearfully and wonderfully made."
- "I am a son or daughter of the King."

Whatever it is, consider it a tender gift from the Creator Himself, spoken directly to you. Because He loves you and wants intimacy with you.

End this exercise with a prayer of gratitude. Thank God for meeting you here, and don't be in a rush to move on to the next thing. Simply sit in the moment with God.

HOW THIS AFFECTS US

When the paths to our hearts are clear and uncluttered, it can provide amazing times of communion with God. Oftentimes the biggest blessings aren't necessarily words or direction, or even answers to our questions, but simply God Himself.

Like Moses as he came down from Sinai[8], we may feel radiant—this is because any encounter with God ignites something deep within; it's that soul place that remembers Eden and longs for its return. When our souls are radiant with the presence of God, our souls are fully alive.

Now, a word of caution.

Sometimes, after an experience with God, we may be inclined to chase the experience rather than chase after God. This is a form of idolatry. If you find yourself drawn in this direction, simply confess this to God, slow down, and sit at His feet. When you do, don't expect anything other than His presence; let that be enough. God's presence is plenty if we allow ourselves the time to slow down and sit with Him expecting nothing other than to simply hear His breath.

My hope is that by incorporating these practices, you begin to find peace—both in God's identity and also who He says you are.

Think about what this could do for your career. Instead of frantically trying to pick the perfect career and putting all kinds of pressure on your choices, a person whose identity is not tied to his or her career will instead live out of a different place—a place where they can be themselves regardless of the context of their vocation. What could your workplace be if it was filled with people who were secure in their identity in Christ, rather than insecure about their identity as a boss, computer coder, fashion designer, or (fill in the blank).

Or how about our relationships?

---

[8] See Exodus 34:29–35.

Instead of basing our self-worth on the number or quality of our friendships or the number of likes or shares on our social platforms, whether or not we are married, have kids, are dating the right person—rather than put all of the pressure on those things—what if we instead rested in who God says we are rather than what those outside influences say about us? Imagine how relaxed (and secure) we might be in our relationships.

Finally, how about our communities?

Based on the above affirmations of career and relationships, we then attach ourselves to various communities—those who self-express in the same way that we do. But since self-expression changes, our communities can then change or become broken which results in us feeling even more unstable, rejected, or outcast.

A person whose identity is rooted in Christ will instead find a community that shares this same common ground of centering itself around Someone that is stable, unchanging, and forever loving. Imagine what community could feel like if we collectively kept Jesus at the center.

The goal here is to make a daily habit of clearing the path to our hearts so that we can remind ourselves of who God is, who He says we are, and then from that place let it permeate outward into our vocation, our relationships, and our communities.

It can truly be a beautiful thing—almost like bringing little pieces of heaven here on earth[9].

---

[9] What Jesus refers to as *The Kingdom of God*. When he often says "the kingdom of God is near", I believe He is referring to these moments when we bring God's glory into these places in our lives and others get the opportunity to see it in action. It's a way "God's bright glory shines" into our spheres of influence.

PART THREE
PUTTING IT ALL TOGETHER

CHAPTER 9

WHAT'S NEXT?

"I am the true grapevine, and my Father is the gardener. He cuts off every branch of mine that doesn't produce fruit, and he prunes the branches that do bear fruit so they will produce even more. You have already been pruned and purified by the message I have given you. Remain in me, and I will remain in you. For a branch cannot produce fruit if it is severed from the vine, and you cannot be fruitful unless you remain in me.

"Yes, I am the vine; you are the branches. Those who remain in me, and I in them, will produce much fruit. For apart from me you can do nothing. Anyone who does not remain in me is thrown away like a useless branch and withers. Such branches are gathered into a pile to be burned. But if you remain in me and my words remain in you, you may ask for anything you want, and it will be granted! When you produce much fruit, you are my true disciples. This brings great glory to my Father.

—John 15:1–8 (NLT)

ABIDING

Imagine you were going away on a dangerous mission and you knew the chances of survival were next to none. In your last evening with your closest friends and family, you would invariably have much to say before you departed, but due to a lack of time, would likely focus on the most important things you wanted to leave them with before you headed out. You might tell them how much they each mean to you, or you might have some instructions to your close friends about how they should take care of your family in your absence. You would likely also have some "*if you remember one thing, remember this*" conversations.

Jesus had similar conversations before He was arrested and brutally murdered, and in one of those conversations, He started talking about vines and branches and fruit. In one of His most famous teachings, Jesus tells His disciples a key *if you remember one thing, remember this* concept:

"*Remain in me.*"

The original language uses the word *abide*[1]–a nuanced word that means to remain, but also implies a certain resolve to stay strong, to stay present, to cling to (in a determined, rather than "clingy" manner).

"*Abide in Me.*"

Stay strong in your resolve and commitment to Me.

Stay present with Me.

---

[1] The Greek word, *Meno*.

WHAT'S NEXT?

Clutch on to Me and hold on for dear life, because when things get tough, you'll need Me.

This "abiding" comes with a promise—we will bear much fruit, and that this fruit will glorify God. It also comes with a warning: If we do not remain in Christ, we can do nothing.

Some of you might push back on that last statement about being able to do nothing, telling me all the things atheists have been able to do for humanity. You might also tell me how dogs help us emotionally even though they don't have the faculties to *abide in Jesus*. I get it. But I think what Jesus is referring to here is that apart from Him, we can't really do anything for the Kingdom. We can't do anything that has a truly eternal impact. We can't, on a soul level, live life to the fullest[2].

But when we *abide* in Jesus, like a branch does with its vine, we have all the sustenance we need and that sustenance provides fullness—both for ourselves and others. There's an implied sense of purpose and meaning when we consider this. For a fruitful life is a purpose-filled life, and a purpose-filled life is a meaningful one.

So how do we abide in Jesus? Let's start by looking at the branches that wither and are ultimately tossed in the fire. Why are they tossed aside? Because they bear no fruit. Why aren't they bearing fruit? Because they have forgotten to abide. What causes them to neglect the abiding?

I would argue the reasons are many, but like the seeds that fall on the thorny soil, they get choked out by the cares and concerns of this world[3]. In other words, when life gets difficult and God suddenly

---

[2] See John 10:10.
[3] See Luke 8:1–15.

doesn't fit into their box, they no longer believe[4]. They didn't have the resolve to clutch onto Jesus with everything they had, holding nothing back, even when things felt hard and out of control.

Before we all rush to judge these folks, let's take an honest look in the mirror and ask ourselves how often we question God when things don't go our way? This is okay, by the way. Read most of the Psalms and you'll see that God can handle these questions. But when the questions feel so big that we no longer trust in the goodness of God, we will find ourselves swimming in some very dangerous waters[5].

The discussion is not whether we should have questions about God (we will, and likely, often); the discussion is about what we do with these questions when they come up. Will we abandon our faith, subtly at first, as we loosen our grip on the Vine? Or will we fight with new resolve, embracing the mystery that is God and His ways, trusting Him even when it feels really difficult to do so? Will we clutch on to Jesus, holding on for dear life, when the storms come and our faith is tested, or will we lose hope and get choked out by the cares and concerns (and worries) of this world?

What about when things are going really well? Perhaps you aren't experiencing a ton of hardship in your current season but instead seem to be blessed with the Midas Touch. All of your work pursuits, relational pursuits, and personal pursuits are all being super successful right now; everything you touch seems to turn to gold. In seasons of prosperity, we can tend to forget our need for Jesus, operating under

---

[4] Refer back to Chapter 7 when a main conflict of belief is that we try to fit God into our box rather than let Him speak for Himself and live outside of any of our boxes.

[5] Every Psalm that begins with questioning God ultimately ends with the declaration of "and yet I will put my trust in you" (or some variation of this); we would do well to remember to land here in times of doubt, resolving to trust even when trust feels really difficult.

the false illusion that all of our blessings come from within, rather than from above. It's why Jesus mused, "how difficult it is for the rich to inherit the kingdom of God[6]"–not impossible, mind you, but difficult. Why? Because when things are going well, we tend to forget God. This is why James, the brother of Jesus, wrote:

> Dear brothers and sisters, when troubles of any kind come your way, consider it an opportunity for great joy. For you know that when your faith is tested, your endurance has a chance to grow. So let it grow, for when your endurance is fully developed, you will be perfect and complete, needing nothing.
>
> —James 1:2–4 (NLT)

No trial or hardship immediately brings forth the feeling of an "opportunity for great joy", but this progression of *trial–testing–endurance-completeness* is a fascinating one. We progress through these trials and navigate these hardships by clinging to Jesus and letting Him carry us through when we don't have the strength to carry on ourselves[7].

The truth is we all want a life of prosperity. But we don't want to have to go through the trials to get there. It's one of the deceits of our modern age–that we can have the prosperity without the trials. But when we live a life with nothing but prosperity we miss out on the trials, and when we miss out on the trials we miss out on the opportunity to learn a greater dependence on Christ.

This is why Jesus' brother says that it can be an opportunity for joy, because when He carries us through the stormy waters and we're on the other side, celebration is in order. When there are no storms

---

[6] See Matthew 19:23.
[7] More on this later. It's gonna blow your mind…

and we forget to acknowledge God's goodness and provision during those times of prosperity, we run the risk of letting the cares and concerns of this world choke us out.

When you're more concerned with growing your own kingdom than God's, you're walking among the thorns; be careful that you don't get too comfortable there.

WHEN WE ABIDE

> "I am praying not only for these disciples but also for all who will ever believe in me through their message. I pray that they will all be one, just as you and I are one—as you are in me, Father, and I am in you. And may they be in us so that the world will believe you sent me.
>
> "I have given them the glory you gave me, so they may be one as we are one. I am in them and you are in me. May they experience such perfect unity that the world will know that you sent me and that you love them as much as you love me.
>
> —John 17:20–23 (NLT)

Okay, enough of the downers. Let's look at what happens when we do abide—when we do choose to hang on, clinging to Jesus at all costs, tapping into His strength when we recognize that we can't do it (whether the "it" is *survive* or *thrive*) on our own.

When we *abide* with Jesus, united with the Vine, we get this beautiful union of God, Jesus, and us. Think about Jesus' prayer for *us*–that we, as followers of Christ because of the faithfulness of the saints who have gone before us, would be united *in Christ*, just as Jesus was united *in the Father*.

Jesus modeled what it was like to *abide* in God—He even says so at the beginning of John 15—and shows us what it looks like to cling in spite of every external circumstance, even death. So when Jesus felt abandoned by God as He hung on the cross, crying out *"my God, my God, why have you abandoned me?*[8]*"* He still chose to abide in the Father and surrender to His plan. If you recall, Jesus could have easily summoned angels and could have avoided the cross altogether. But because of Jesus' resolve to cling to the Father at all costs, you and I have access to life to the fullest—all because Jesus modeled what *abiding* looks like.

When we abide in Jesus, we abide in God. When we choose not to abide in Jesus, we place our dependence on ourselves and in doing so, reject dependence on God (which is rejecting God). Do we see the stakes here? We can have access to the very glory of God Himself—*if* we abide in Jesus.

These were some of His last words before He was hauled off and arrested so we would do well to take them with the same measure of importance that Jesus offered them in.

BACK TO IDENTITY

This *abiding* in Jesus unites us with Him, and by extension, unifies us with God. If we have placed God as central, taking His identity for who He says He is, we can then allow who God says *we* are to take root. When our lives are ordered in this manner, the result is *abundance*, a *full life*, and *much fruit*.

---

[8] See Matthew 27:46.

When we allow our lives to become disordered and begin walking among the thorns, we loosen our grip on Jesus, and we become more formed by the world than we are formed by Jesus. We may feel a small burst of abundance, but it will fade over time. We may feel full for a moment, but then emptiness will creep in; we may feel like we are successful, but the fruit we bear will not last. We will have replaced the Infinite with things that are finite. Like the woman at the well, we drink from water that makes us thirsty again. Jesus offers another way.

This all stems from our core; where we place our identity is a direct result of whom we have chosen to abide with–have we chosen Jesus, or have we chosen ourselves?

How, then, do we abide? Let's revisit Isaiah 40.

BACK TO THE BEGINNING

> Thunder in the desert!
> "Prepare for God's arrival!
> Make the road straight and smooth,
> a highway fit for our God.
> Fill in the valleys,
> level off the hills,
> Smooth out the ruts,
> clear out the rocks.
> Then God's bright glory will shine
> and everyone will see it.
> Yes. Just as God has said."
>
> Isaiah 40:3–5 (MSG)

> But those who wait upon God get fresh strength.
> They spread their wings and soar like eagles,
> They run and don't get tired,
> they walk and don't lag behind.
>
> Isaiah 40:31 (MSG)

Isaiah 40 ends with a beautiful promise. Those who wait on God will get fresh strength. They will run and not get tired; they will walk and not lag behind. *They will soar.*

Sounds a little like the apostle Paul, doesn't it, when he says he has run the race well[9]? Doesn't a little *fresh strength* sound like water to your thirsty soul? In times like the ones we're living in, we all need more strength, we all need more endurance, we all need more hope to keep carrying on. In times like these, that strength, endurance, and hope are so desperately needed inside us so that we can also offer those qualities to others. We can learn to offer the hope we have to a world that has lost its hope. We can endure because we have strength.

How do we get this strength? How do we soar like eagles?

We wait upon God.

Now, here's where it gets so wonderfully mind-blowing:

The Hebrew word used here for "wait" is *qavah*.

Do you know what that word translates to in English?

Abide.

---

[9] See 2 Timothy 4:7.

Abide in God. Cling to Him with everything you've got–during the good times, during the bad times. During the times of prosperity and the times of trial. Fight with all you've got to stay connected with God, and during the storms, when all hope seems to be lost, when desperation sets in, your act of *abiding* will be your lifeblood.

It will be your source of hope.

You will be given fresh strength.

You will soar.

CHAPTER 10

CONCLUSION

MORE ON EMMANUEL

How many times do we find ourselves praying, "Lord, be with me today" or, "Father, be with Susie today as she's in her job interview", or any other variation of the "Lord be with" kinds of prayers. I have been in all kinds of church circles where these are the prayers we offer up. In fact, I probably prayed a similar prayer already this morning: *"Lord, be with my wife on her day off; may it be a recharging and refreshing day for her."*

Maybe those are the wrong prayers.

Now don't get me wrong—there is something beautiful about lifting one another up in prayer, about considering the lives of others, and about inviting God's presence to dwell among His people. This is one of the many reasons why Christian community is so valuable—we need others in our lives to see us, to speak into our lives, to pray with and for us. I just wonder if part of our prayers are ever so slightly misguided.

If we know and trust that God is *with us*, we don't need to be asking Him to *join us*. He's already there. Maybe a better prayer looks something like: "Jesus, I know you're here with me; may I be reminded of that throughout my day".

How could the simplicity of that prayer change your whole perspective? Its implications are so simple, and yet so significant.

Operating under the baseline that we already know Jesus is *with us*, what could divine reminders of that presence do for our souls?

I would argue that we have these divine reminders all the time, but by praying that prayer, it helps us tune into God's presence throughout the day. It helps us to be more mindful of the little blessings and the maybe not-so-little provisions that God provides throughout each day.

Maybe it's as simple as a bird singing in a tree after a rainstorm, and maybe that bird conveys the message that God has provided for this small animal even through the stormy seasons of life, and that because it knows it's provided for, it can sing a tune, celebrating the passing of the storm. That bird that you would have possibly ignored, or at best appreciated its tune, now has deeper implications for your own life as you notice the stress you're carrying about work, about your finances, and about the security of your future. A prayer asking God to remind you of His presence suddenly transforms a singing bird into a reminder of the promise that God is never going to leave you nor forsake you[1].

The truth is, God is always with us, and the best way to recognize that, to be in tune with His presence, is to work on daily clearing the path to our hearts. One of the ways we clear the path is simply to invite God to reveal Himself throughout our day. It helps us to be more intentionally mindful about His presence, and that

---

[1] See Jeremiah 29:11.

mindfulness opens our eyes and our hearts to the incredible blessings all around us.

It helps us engage with *Emmanuel*–God with us.

Now, I know that for many Christians, we have been ingrained to think of God as "out there", so this approach will require quite a bit of reprogramming in our minds and in our hearts. But if we've learned anything from this daily practice of clearing the path, it's that it's possible, and it invites God into the process, providing more relational intimacy and therefore carrying the potential of filling our hearts to overflowing.

How might our lives look different if we did the work to change our perspective on this?

Dallas Willard was once giving a lecture to a room of college students. He began by asking them, *If you could use only one word to describe Jesus, what would it be?* Words came out from among the students like: *holy, glorious, sacrificial,* and so on.

If you were to answer that question for yourself, what would you say? Likely some of the above, as well as other true characteristics of Jesus; the list could easily be quite long.

After hearing these responses, Willard affirmed all of them, and then offered his own thought on the question: "If I could use one word to describe Jesus, it would be… *relaxed.*" The students laughed, but then he went on to explain how, when we're sure of our identity, when we're present to the moment, when we're in the exact place we know we're supposed to be, when we know beyond a shadow of doubt that we are living out our purpose and calling, we are *relaxed*.

Willard went on to argue that Jesus was the most relaxed person in the history of humankind. Jesus knew God's identity. Jesus knew His own identity (as confirmed by the Father). Based on these two characteristics, Jesus knew how to be in the moment, not getting ahead of Himself because He knew He was living out His calling and was in the exact place He was supposed to be. He knew He was living the most meaningful life ever lived.

How was He so certain of this? Think about how many times Jesus regularly withdrew by Himself to pray[2]. I think if Jesus, as the perfect man, knew the importance of regularly connecting in intimate ways with God, we would do well to imitate that pattern. And we do that, of course, by clearing the path, so that we can enjoy connecting with the Father.

Much can be said about Jesus withdrawing to pray, and I think when we consider this pattern we can sometimes forget that, although Jesus was fully God, He was also fully human. But even in that *fully human* state, Jesus *knew* that God was with him. Always.

Not "up there", but *with*.

As we adjust our prayers to remind ourselves that God is *with* rather than *out*, a natural byproduct will be that we will become more relaxed. Relaxed as we recognize who God is and reorient our lives to keep Him at the center. Relaxed as we recognize who we are, because we have allowed God to speak into our identity rather than carrying the burdens of trying to self-express an identity independent of God. Relaxed as we, operating out of a place where God is at the center, and out of a place where we understand that our truest identity is in

---

[2] See Luke 5:16 as well as countless other places in Scripture where Jesus withdrew from the crowds to find "lonely places" to pray and connect with the Father.

CONCLUSION

Christ[3], can then experience the joy of a meaningful and fulfilled life, because we have experienced God's best for us. We, in our frail humanity, can become imitators of Christ, and can therefore be more relaxed on a deep, core level.

We can become people whose *very souls* are… relaxed.

When I look at the world around me, I don't see a whole lot of relaxed people. Even the people who are supposed to be relaxing are busy posting all of their relaxation online so that other people can know how relaxed they are while they scurry on their phones, managing the likes and comments and shares. This is not evidence of a soul that is relaxed. But what could it look like for *you* to have a soul that is relaxed? As you consider your sphere, your work and your relationships, what would a relaxed soul do for you? I believe that part of the key to unlocking a relaxed soul is by daily reminding ourselves that God is truly with us.

And it starts with that slight adjustment to our morning prayers:

> *Jesus, remind me of Your presence with me today. When I forget (because I'm prone to forget), gently remind me that You are here, with me, in all of my comings and goings, in all of my conversations, and in all of the pleasant and unpleasant parts of my day.*
>
> *Help me be tuned in to Your presence with me, amen.*

---

[3] For a great read on the topic, grab a copy of *You Are Not Your Own* by Alan Noble.

WALKING IN THE CLEAR PATH

I believe that God has an adventure for us all to live. I believe He is able to accomplish far more than we can ever imagine in us and through us[4]. I also believe that as humans we settle for far less. To grasp hold of the life that Jesus has for us requires incredible effort, incredible discipline, and ultimate submission to Him and His plan for our lives. And that plan is almost always filled with seasons of murkiness, where our sight is unclear and we aren't able to skip to the last chapter, reading ahead in our stories to see where the whole thing is going.

But the more that I've practiced submitting to God's plan by working hard to keep the path to my heart clear, the more I realize that no, God is not safe; but He is good. In His goodness, I have begun to experience glimpses of that "exceedingly more than we can hope or imagine" kind of life. It truly is rooted in Jesus' words where anyone who wants to find his life must lose it for His sake[5]; the more I have released control and sought after God's direction, submitting to His plans, the more I have experienced life to the full–and isn't that the beautiful promise of Jesus?

What could our workplaces look like if they were filled with people whose souls were relaxed and who enjoyed living life to the full? Full of meaning and purpose? Full of God? What could our communities look like? What about our churches? Could we, through clearing the path in our hearts, be agents of change and healing and *life* in those spheres God has placed us in? It starts by preparing the way. It continues by remembering who God is, and clinging to who He says we are.

---

[4] See Ephesians 3:20.
[5] See Matthew 16:25.

CONCLUSION

It is sustainable by learning to rest in Jesus' presence, being filled by Him, and thus waiting on, and *abiding in*, the Lord. We will be filled with fresh strength and ultimately soar as we live out of a place where our soul is filled with the very presence of God.

And so my challenge is this:

Put these things into practice. If you're unsure, give it one month. If that's too difficult, give it a week. See if you notice any changes in your soul. And then tell others about it. Or better yet, tell *me* about it[6].

Because the world needs more people who have come alive–especially at a time like this.

The track near my house is still not finished. In fact, the workers have had to unearth more boulders from beneath the dirt, heaping them in new piles off to the side of the track. Clearly, there is much work still to be done. But like the work in progress that is *us*, I fast forward in my mind to a day when the track is finished and pristine, filled with students running their events, friends and parents cheering them on as they give their all in the races.

The track will come to life as it is used for the purpose its designers had for it.

And at that moment, all of the hard work of filling valleys, removing hills, filling ruts and clearing out the rocks will have been utterly and completely worth it …

---

[6] Seriously: email me at nathan.a.westwick@gmail.com and I will personally respond to you.

When I think of all this, I fall to my knees and pray to the Father, the Creator of everything in heaven and on earth. I pray that from his glorious, unlimited resources he will empower you with inner strength through his Spirit. Then Christ will make his home in your hearts as you trust in him. Your roots will grow down into God's love and keep you strong. And may you have the power to understand, as all God's people should, how wide, how long, how high, and how deep his love is. May you experience the love of Christ, though it is too great to understand fully. Then you will be made complete with all the fullness of life and power that comes from God.

Now all glory to God, who is able, through his mighty power at work within us, to accomplish infinitely more than we might ask or think. Glory to him in the church and in Christ Jesus through all generations forever and ever! Amen.

—Ephesians 3:14–21 (NLT)

BENEDICTION

May the God who is bigger than all governments, bigger than all armies, bigger than all political and social systems–may the God who created life, conquered death, and restores humanity–may this God bless you and keep you as you learn to rest in His presence. And as you do, may your heart be filled with peace, may your life be one of holy adventure, and may those who have the privilege of crossing your path be inspired by God's Spirit living in you so that they may be curious about this God who has given you peace, comfort, security, and hope. May you, by living out your purpose, draw others closer to the Kingdom.

For the glory of God, and for the betterment of the world. Amen.

AFTERWORD

Writing this book was a spiritual high. The intimacy I felt with God as He and I partnered to write this was one of the most richly fulfilling experiences I've had the pleasure to enjoy.

Since then, in the months that have followed, life has gotten ... *dull*.

Or maybe a better way to describe it would be that life has been filled with all kinds of challenges. Relational. Financial. Spiritual. Anything but the full, abundant life I wrote about just a few pages ago.

Friends, this is real life.

Sometimes you're sitting with friends and family, enjoying laughter, togetherness, and the finest of meals, and other times you're battling loneliness, fatigue, and struggling to find any kind of meal that will satisfy. I have had many a weary moment since finishing this book. And it all came to a head this morning when, at a very low moment, I wasn't sure what was true any more. Do my friends love me? Does my wife love me? And the worst: Does *God* love me?

Is my life going anywhere, or am I going to keep stalling out, taking one step forward and two steps back for the rest of my waking days? Am I an imposter, having finished a book about clearing the path, accessing incredible intimacies with God the Father, with Jesus, and with the Holy Spirit, only to struggle living it out on my own, despite my best efforts?

As I recently told my spiritual director, I'm doing all the right things: I'm not making a habit of engaging in sinful behavior, I'm practicing Sabbath, I'm reading the Bible and praying every morning, and yet I still feel incredibly dry. His advice? Work to be attentive to where God is, and follow Him there. If He moves, follow Him there; if He stays, sit with Him there. Don't get ahead of Him, don't get behind Him; seek Him and go wherever He is.

So I have genuinely tried to do that. I have been reading Exodus, paying attention to the pillar of smoke and the cloud of fire. I have been earnestly seeking God, trying diligently to keep the path clear. And yet the path doesn't feel clear. My life has still been stormy, rocky, unsettled, and disrupted.

And if I'm honest, there's nothing quite as discouraging as feeling like you're doing all of the right things and progressing to absolutely nowhere. Especially if you just wrote a book about all the things we can do to enjoy Emmanuel—the presence of God with us in our everyday life, transforming our potentially dull lives into lives that are rich, full, and dynamic.

But the truth is, heaven isn't always present on Earth.

But the other truth? *God is.*

───

This morning has felt particularly low. I tried jump-starting my morning with coffee; I still felt tired. I moved on to more of Exodus; it felt bland. I cried out to God; it felt lonely and dispassionate. I headed over to the gym; I didn't feel revitalized. I tried numbing out on Instagram, wrestling with whether I wanted to spend too much time there, potentially going down a dangerous rabbit hole that could result in me doing things I would later need to confess to my wife. I chose not to.

Or maybe, more accurately, God gave me the strength to choose not to. But just before I closed the app, I re-checked our company's feed of likes and shares. There was a new follower with a last name that sounded vaguely familiar, like a blast from the past. Above that notification was a "like" from someone with the same last name; probably a brother or husband. I recognized his name. It was a former student of mine, when I taught middle school, 22 years ago. I clicked on his profile, maybe secretly hoping to find pics of him living some idealized lifestyle that would make me feel jealous and unaccomplished. It was definitely my former student, and he had no pictures of any romanticized life; just normal, real adventures he had taken with his wife, out Jeeping in nature and playing in the snow.

I scrolled further, and saw a quote he had reposted. It read:

> "Not all storms come to disrupt your life, some come to clear your path."

I paused. I uttered under my breath, then read it again. And then I thought to myself: *of* all *the places, God ... I haven't heard this kid's name in over 20 years. I don't know if he's even a follower of Jesus, and yet here he posts a random quote that reminds me, even when I'm feeling at my lowest, that You are here with me.*

You see me.

You still love me.

You will always be here with me; You will never leave me; You will always keep pursuing me.

Friends, sometimes *abiding* is much easier said than done. Even when we are resolved to cling on tightly with all that we have, sometimes our own strength falls painfully short. But there have been times in my life, thanks be to God, when my own efforts and strengths fail me and the storms of life leave me feeling battered, weary, and about to let go and about to give up hope. In those moments, God is there to catch me, to hold me, and to remind me of His presence. And I have to be honest: That reminder this morning has not changed my circumstances surrounding my day. I am still anxious about the relational struggles I face. I am still anxious about the financial struggles I face. I don't know how the script is going to play out. I don't know what stories I'll be telling a month from now, or a year from now.

But I do know this: God, in His gentle but relentless pursuit of me, has given me *fresh strength* this morning. And here's what I'm learning: At times, the *abiding* is much more difficult than we might think. It might cost us much more than we are ready to offer. It might challenge us more than we are ready for, surfacing things that bring about toil, pain, and suffering. The *waiting* can be much longer than we might prefer. Sometimes, just when we've carried more than we think we are able, and the storms are just about to take us out …

God shows up. And the very act of Him showing up gives us strength to keep going.

If you're facing storms right now, and you're trying all the right things but they don't seem to be working, don't lose heart. Keep pursuing God. Keep working to clear your path. Keep asking, keep knocking, keep seeking. Because when the time is right, *He will show up.*

And when He does, He promises to give us fresh strength. Not necessarily *deliverance*, but *strength*. When He does show up, I pray that it recharges you, refuels you, and revitalizes you to keep on keeping on, enjoying those moments with God, even if (and as) their timing might surprise us.

May you be filled with fresh strength even today …

ACKNOWLEDGMENTS

If you find anything impactful from this book, all glory goes to God, who, during one of my morning prayer times gave me a vivid picture in my head of a freshly-paved, wide road stretched out in the desert. A few days later I happened upon Isaiah 40 which blew my mind, as it described in detail the picture God had given me earlier. I asked God if I should write a book about it, and He said *yes*.

I am incredibly grateful for my wife, Laurel, and three sons, Garrett, Emmett, and Abbott, for keeping my life full and rich and wonderful. You all are the joy of my life and I thank God for you daily. I am so incredibly blessed to get to live life with you all. Laurel, your wisdom, support, and spiritual counsel enrich me in so many ways. Boys, I am so incredibly proud of each of you; you are all truly wonderful young men.

To my parents, who had the courage to come to faith in Jesus at a critical season in their lives, and for sharing that faith with my brother and me.

To my home church, Sandals Church, for giving me a place to serve and explore my calling. To Pastor Matt Brown, for taking the time to be God's instrument in pulling me out of a very dark period all those years ago. To Dan Crowley for seeing that God had a purpose for me when I couldn't see it myself, and for your faithful and patient discipleship of me over the years. It is truly a joy and a privilege to work alongside you and to call you a friend.

To my spiritual director, James Mitchell, who points out what God is up to when I am prone to miss it. Your incredible wisdom has influenced this book more than you know.

To Brett Ryan, the world's best therapist and a brilliant man. I am truly grateful for you.

To Wild Goose Coffee Roasters for keeping me well-fueled with really tasty caffeine all these years. To Chris Richey who ran the business while I wrote this book.

To Tyler Bianco, whose editing experience was an answer to prayer.

To those friends in my life who, over the years, kept encouraging me to write; you know who you are and I am truly blessed by you. A special shout-out to The Fellas, who love and support me because of who I am, and not because of anything you gain in your friendship with me. You all have been such an incredible blessing over the years; thank you. To Dave and Melanie, I can truly be myself around you guys; thank you for your sustained friendship and for being amazing traveling companions!

To my community group, you have been such a bright spot in Laurel's and my life; we are so humbled that you would come to our house each week to open up your lives to us all, sharing personal stories of how God is working, and for being a place of faithful and encouraging prayer.

Lastly, to you, for taking a chance on reading this book. My prayer for this book has been that it would land on the hearts of those who need to hear it. I pray that, just maybe, that might have happened with you, and that God might have used this to bring you one step closer to Him.

If this book somehow encouraged you in your faith journey and brought you ever so slightly closer to Jesus, I would consider it my incredible reward.

And now to Him who is able to accomplish infinitely more than we could ever hope or imagine; may His glory fill the earth; may His followers be many, and may they experience, deep within their souls, meaning, purpose, and intimacy with the good, gracious, patient, and loving Father. Amen.

ABOUT THE AUTHOR

Nathan Westwick lives with his wife of 24 years and his three teenage sons in the Redlands, CA area. He is a licensed minister and works in the Spiritual Formation ministry at Sandals Church, a multi-site church in Southern California, leading teams who produce content aimed at bringing people closer to Jesus. In addition to his ministry at the church, Nathan is a business owner (Wild Goose Coffee Roasters) and former math teacher (Yucaipa High School–his alma mater).

To read his thoughts on balancing faith, family, and business, visit his blog at lifetakesfaith.com. For info on his business, visit wildgoosecoffee.com. To engage with the Sandals Church content, including several interactive Bible reading plans, please visit the church app at sandalschurch.com/app.

Printed in the USA
CPSIA information can be obtained
at www.ICGtesting.com
LVHW051927220823
755797LV00009B/23/J